David,
I hope you find as
much meaning in my
story as I have in yours.
Thank you for sharing
your gifts of spirit.

Skip (foyd)

2019

Find Your Bridge

Jayd Jarrett

BALBOA.
PRESS
A DIVISION OF HAY HOUSE

Balboa Press books may be ordered through booksellers or by contacting:

Balboa Press
A Division of Hay House
1663 Liberty Drive
Bloomington, IN 47403
www.balboapress.com
1 (877) 407-4847

Because of the dynamic nature of the Internet, any web addresses or links contained in this book may have changed since publication and may no longer be valid. The views expressed in this work are solely those of the author and do not necessarily reflect the views of the publisher, and the publisher hereby disclaims any responsibility for them.

The author of this book does not dispense medical advice or prescribe the use of any technique as a form of treatment for physical, emotional, or medical problems without the advice of a physician, either directly or indirectly. The intent of the author is only to offer information of a general nature to help you in your quest for emotional and spiritual well-being. In the event you use any of the information in this book for yourself, which is your constitutional right, the author and the publisher assume no responsibility for your actions.

Any people depicted in stock imagery provided by Thinkstock are models, and such images are being used for illustrative purposes only. Certain stock imagery © Thinkstock.

Print information available on the last page.

ISBN: 978-1-5043-3231-6 (sc)
ISBN: 978-1-5043-3232-3 (e)

Library of Congress Control Number: 2015906867

Balboa Press rev. date: 05/20/2015

Acknowledgements

I am ever grateful to every family member and friend mentioned in this book. Names, places and other identifying details have been changed to protect individual privacy, but you know who you are. I wouldn't be here without you. Thank you for your patience with me, your help, and your love. I adore you.

I am in awe, still, of the divine intervention that came through me in the form of alters and guides. You brought great healing and peace, as you promised.

Thank you to McKenna Donovan, my intuitive and generous editor, who believed in my words and helped guide the process professionally and compassionately.

Introduction

Find Your Bridge details one year of my life. Only one amazing, unforgettable year that changed everything for me forever, and for many others as well. It's all true. I couldn't have made it up. I'm not that creative.

It has taken years for me to gather enough insight and knowledge to even begin to understand all that we experienced. But the time has come for the telling, and I have done my best with it.

Everyone's names are changed for their privacy, as are specific details and locations. These wonderful people deserve to be recognized, but some are traveling in other directions now.

"Thom" and my parents particularly deserve more credit than they receive within these pages. At the time, my perspective was years younger and much more narrow. I know now how very much they gave me. We all make choices in our lives that we wish we could change. They contributed as much, or even more, to the power of the messages in this book as the rest of us. We all help each other to find our bridges. In their own ways, they gave of themselves to do that for me. They made me stronger and more confident in the end. I loved them when that miraculous year began. I love them still.

You are about to meet "alters" and "guides." Liza is one of them. These are the multiple personalities and mystical "Others" who came with healing and love. They are still a mystery to me.

Read with an open heart and mind. My hope is that within the story, you will see how your own journey is guided with purpose and love. No matter how it appears. We all help each other to be better. Don't judge the path, just follow it to your bridge.

Liza

I bid you welcome. My name is Liza. I am an aspect and an alter. One of many who once spoke through the body of Rebecca. We rose within her because she let us. In fact, she called to us from the heart and we heard her. And Others heard as well. Others who live in realms unknown here in this flat and frozen world of grief. And how you do grieve. You grieve your losses and your failures, your broken hearts and dreams. You grieve your lack and even your love. You lose your way within it.

I am here to tell you in your words what it is like, living apart from grief and loss. And what it is like to come home. It is clear, unburdened and free. It is all things and all ways and all of the All. We lived across the bridge before we were summoned here. Each of us a thought in the mind of God; a rhythm, a wave, a blending of souls. And when we came here, we breathed through Rebecca and we shared her ways and her pain. And we taught her how to heal and how to thin her earthly essence and how to move out of the way for her truth. It hurt her, this truth of your world, but it healed her, too, in the end. And when Jayd came to discover herself, we were there for her as well.

I promised I would return to help write her story and to share with all what it takes for a lost one to find their bridge. It takes belief... in the reality of things unseen and in nudges from inside that can come only from a Power so great that it can change the past, the present and the future. As you would turn your face to the sun on a cold day, she turned toward that Power. And it came to her as she asked. It came from within – as it must. I came, and Lynn, Cassie, Peter Pan and Amelia of the Path. We all came to help her.

And the Others, the guides, came with us. They brought great insights and gifts from the Power. They brought light... not to chase the darkness, but to claim it. For within this darkness lay great gifts of peace and love and truth; the truth of their existence and their presence in the world. They are. We are. Just as you are.

Your guides come to you from within as they must. They speak your language, they do not exceed your ability to understand, and they fulfill promises in distinctly and uniquely your own voice. They help you to seek and to see what you have not seen. They bring your attention to those things of the world that are not as they appear to the darkened eye. When it is your time to awaken and find your bridge, they will come to you, as you ask them. There are multitudes of helpers. Yours is not a voice alone. You are always heard, and you are answered according to your ability to receive and accept. It is our hope that you will ask and that when your help comes, you will not judge, compare, or desire to change its form into the familiar. Be vigilant and listen. We will not fight for silence.

Hear her story. Understand that its truths are yours as well.

Jayd

This story is true, every word as it was spoken years ago. It has taken many years to understand its depth, meaning, and purpose. It began when, in desperation, a wife and mother named Rebecca cried, "God, there has to be a better way! Please just give me peace." And in response, she heard clearly the words, "Let it go." Just like that. "Let it go."

So she did, over the next year. She let go of control and expectations and assumptions about herself and her life. She let go of an image, actually, because that's really all it was. Fiction. And you can't be truly happy and free, if you're living a false life.

And all this matters because she was not so different from you. You yearn for happiness and love. You do your best in life. You try to believe in something greater than yourself. And you pretend.

"Let it go" are profoundly empowering words and very difficult to do. But if you are ever to release what is not yours to bear, to claim something greater than just a dream, to walk your bridge from here to happiness, you must let go of what binds you from within. For it is within your mind that you struggle, while your heart and soul know the truth.

I ask you to walk with me, and with Liza, as we introduce you to Rebecca and show you how one life collapses so that another may begin. In letting go, Rebecca discovered that life begins within. It may have been two souls changing places. It may have been a divine encounter with an oversoul. It may have all been imagination, but the result was incredible. Rebecca became Jayd. And now, as Jayd, I am overwhelmed with the great joy that has been given me and forever grateful that I was allowed this journey with these people. It is precious to me.

Throughout Rebecca's story, Liza and I will provide insights and observations that could only come from making it to the bridge. You will find that Liza is not who she was when the story began, but neither am I... nor are you. We evolve, learn, grow. That's creation.

My hope is that as you travel these pages you will find the treasures hidden in your own life. That you will turn your attention within and listen, acknowledge, receive and evolve. Accept and connect to a power so great that it can change time.

Liza and I can't explain the magic. No one can. And we can't walk your path for you. You must find your own bridge in your own way. But we can show you how we did it and, in that, let you know it can be done. And when you find your bridge, may it bring you peace... as it has for us.

The Journey Begins:
Running Away

I find solitude in the secluded spare room of our spacious house where I light candles and seek answers. The gloom of the cold April day settles in as tonight, curled into myself on the old flowered couch, I come to the end of it. There is no marriage left, no words to save us this time. I give up. I am letting go in faith that it is the right thing to do. My heart knows it's best, my head is not so sure.

There is no sign of spring, no robins or warmth, and no acknowledgement from Thom when I say I'm leaving with our daughters. He doesn't believe me and he has every reason not to. I've threatened to go many times for many reasons. He listens to my words, but he doesn't agree, and he leaves any compromising to me.

I tell him that in a week we will leave him in this home that has been ours for only two years. It was to be our new beginning in the country. Five wooded acres, a creek, and a beautiful, expansive, dream home that I thought would save us. As I look into his eyes for the first time in weeks, I hope for a change or warmth, but I see nothing new.

We move tomorrow, so I spend today sorting and separating. He joins me at the table while our two girls pack upstairs. I look up into his crystal blue eyes and I can't help myself.

"Please meet me half way! This isn't what I wanted. Tell me how to save us. Tell me you want us to stay." He hesitates and then goes down on one knee before me and then lowers the other to the floor. With moist eyes he whispers, "I'm sorry I can't be who you want me to be. I am who I am."

He leaves the house early the next morning. He has chosen. Our closest friends Sean and Molly come to help me move. They have chosen, too. We'll be okay, I promise the girls. We'll have all-night chats and popcorn fights and picnics on the bed. No more anger, struggle or conflict.

Lee, at sixteen, is mature and insightful, independent, tall and model-thin. Large hazel eyes reveal every thought, and the one childlike dimple in her cheek when she smiles makes her look sweeter than she would like. Her smile will light a room and, if provoked, her temper will clear it. Elizabeth is twelve, and her generous heart beats with love and sentimentality. Her button nose with a wide bridge gives her big blue eyes a sweet innocence. When she was very small, she sang happy little tunes that were born in her heart. As she grew, those melodies drifted to me in the mornings before school or softly from the back seat of the car. But there has been no sweet voice singing in this house.

Looking Back

We've moved into the first floor of a faded pink Victorian farmhouse resting quietly behind some trees on the edge of town. The girls each have a bedroom and I sleep on a daybed in the living room. There are two occupied apartments above and one below and it's shabby compared to what we left behind, but it's ours.

I am alone for the first time in my life. No, not alone. I have my girls. Lee came after three years of marriage when Thom and I were 25. When we were 29, his mother died unexpectedly. Elizabeth was born just weeks later. Then, within two months, his father, broken-hearted and recovering from a previous illness, also passed away. The girls and I were not enough to ease Thom's pain. It was too great a loss and he escaped it in ways that did not include us.

I watch the streetlights through the frilly sheer curtains on the windows across from my bed. It's quiet and the girls are settled for the night. Footsteps recede upstairs and our neighbor's day is done. I am left alone with the darkness, the emptiness, and the doubt. What will I do without him? And now, as I sit in silence, childhood memories surface from the deep. As though I don't have enough going on in my heart. I can't sleep and food doesn't interest me. I'm overwhelmed by the present, and now much too full of the past as well.

The girls and I spend evenings now with Sean and Molly. I'm drawn to their little house a few miles away where they laugh and play and only clear the clutter when they feel like it. We've been friends for over 20 years; a true testament that opposites do attract. Sean is easy-going and comfortable, a steady light in the storm. And Molly is uninhibited and haphazard, fun and fearless. Their home is chaotic, full of noise and enthusiasm. Their nearly 12-year-old daughter Ann, the dancer, acrobat, and constant whirlwind, is always the center of attention. But visiting our friends so much in the two weeks since we moved has been difficult for Elizabeth, whose empathic ability makes her sensitive to the almost constant commotion. The home she knows was orderly, quiet and predictable. Stuffy, in fact. But now, for me, being with my friends is liberating. They don't care about messes or rules. I feel accepted and safe here. My girls want to create a new life of our own but I can't stay away. As long as I have these friends, I might make it another day.

As the days slowly pass toward June, however, the mirror won't keep my secrets. It tells on me. The hours awake in the night, the little food I've been able to tolerate. It shows. I am thinning and haggard. My life force draining from a slow leak in my heart.

I try my best to maintain, though, for the girls and for me. Walking and talking with Sean and Molly after work on the dusty road that leads to their house soothes me. I gain new realizations about my marriage. He and I were good together in many ways and I thought we had it all under control. In public, we were the perfect image of a perfect family. Thom's business was going well, our daughters excelled in school, we enjoyed a comfortable lifestyle, and we were involved in the community. Privately, though, our relationship was confusing. His touch eased my body, but not my soul. He respected me, yet he didn't. He was devoted to me, yet he wasn't. He indulged me, yet he didn't. He loved me...

Checking Out

On a warm Sunday, the second week of June, Sean and I drive to my little cottage on the lake where some of the best days of my marriage were spent. Sean generously offers his day off, and his truck, to help me sort and organize stuff and memories. After I filed for divorce, Thom and I agreed that he will keep the house and I'll take over payments on the cottage. We bought it a few years ago because it was close to Sean's family's cottage on another lake only a couple miles away. Many weekends were spent traveling between their beach and ours. Campfires, pontoon floats, the girls clinging to tubes dragged behind their speeding bass boat. So many good times now gone.

I am here to sell the pontoon today, to mow the lawn and clean out the refrigerator. I have to decide what stays and what goes. I have to remember. I have to forget.

I sit for a minute in the sunroom staring through the trees, recalling my girls' happy laughter as they tossed balls into the water for the dog to chase. They dip for minnows and catch sunfish. They meet other kids from around the lake and play in the sand. I drift with these memories beyond the leafy branches of white birch trees, over the lake and into the blue of the sky. I am no longer earthbound and worn. Time swirls in slow motion along with my thoughts and I savor the moment.

"Hey! Come on!!" It's Sean, shaking my shoulders.

"What's wrong?" I ask as I try to focus again.

"You scared the shit out of me, that's what!"

"Huh?"

"I couldn't get you to respond to me! I tried to talk to you, but you wouldn't answer. You were just... gone!"

Later, with the cottage closed and locked, I make my way to the truck, exhausted and overwhelmed. In shock, actually, that this disintegration of my life is really happening. And I still can't quite get myself out of the sunroom and back into the moment.

On the drive home, Sean asks how I feel about men and dating in the future. Ugh! Disgust and fear roll through me at the thought of dating.

"Men are powerful and they hurt you," I say.

The next morning I drag myself to work on unsteady legs. Yesterday's trip took its toll and I'm still a depleted mess, and my mind won't work. I struggle with the blurred print on the papers on my desk and have to give up after only 20 minutes. I can't force myself to work today. I ask for, and receive, sick time and take the half-hour drive home in a pouring rain. I need help. I can't pull myself together, food is tasteless, and the nights are way too long. The burden of living alone, being alone, providing alone, deciding alone... is a nightmare for me. When I married, I was still living with my parents. I paid for college so they let me live with them rent-free. I had not dated before Thom. I had not partied. I had no real independence and now it's catching up with me. But I'm the smart one, right? I'm the steady, reliable one. The one who takes care of others. So why is this so hard for me?

The girls are stretched out in front of the TV and obviously surprised to see me come in. They don't ask questions, though, when I get on the phone.

"I'm making an appointment with Dr. Henry," I say lightly. He's been our family doctor for years. "And a girl at work told me about a therapist that helped with her divorce so I'm calling her for an appointment. You go ahead and watch your show." I quietly make my calls and I'm amazed that both doctors have open appointments tomorrow. But when I hang up, the girls are paying more attention than I would like.

"So, Lee, are you ready for your trip next week? Are you excited? I'm so proud of you! I'll take that day off work to drive you. You'll have so much fun!"

Lee, as one of the top students in the county, was selected to attend a two-week multicultural program at the university. It's a huge accomplishment for a high school sophomore and it will be great for her to get away for a while.

"Yeah, Mom, I'll be ready," she tells me, but I don't think I'm fooling her.

And now it's Tuesday and I don't know how I'll get through the rest of the week. Each day sucks more life from me. I don't understand. I have a good job with this company, with great pay and benefits. I can make it on my own. I can pay my bills. I'll be fine. I'll be okay. I will.

I take a morning break with Angie in the cafeteria. She works in the cubicle next to me and knows how my marriage has decayed over the past year. She calls Thom a troll and makes me laugh. But she's young and single and independent and I'm not sure she really understands why this is so hard for me. Why I'm not happy to be free of him. But Angie has her own house, and an independent life, and strong opinions. She has no man to tell her what to do, how to do it, when to do it. She doesn't know about married life. My father was in charge when I was a kid. My husband was in charge in my marriage. That's reality.

Later, in the office of our family doctor, I tell him how challenging life has become, but he can see that for himself. I look like hell. I've obviously lost weight and I'm sure I look as fragile as I feel.

"I'm taking you off work the rest of the week." He says. "You need to eat... and sleep."

Then he hands me some Paxil samples and tells me how many to take, but his words don't make sense. I can't get them straight in my mind.

"What?"

"Go home! Get some rest and come back in two days," he calls on his way to the next patient.

That's it? But I'm not better. I can't... I'm not okay. Maybe if I eat. I stop at a McDonald's drive-through and then drive straight to Sean and Molly's. I need to... have to. No one is here, but the door is unlocked so I assume Molly will be back soon and I step through the swinging café doors into the kitchen. The bright orange countertops are cluttered with random objects as usual. It's strangely quiet and even peaceful as I unwrap my sandwich. But my hands shake badly and the smell of the hamburger turns my stomach. God, Rebecca, get a grip! I fumble with the package of Paxil and choke down two pills. Is that what the doctor said? Take two? Or one. Two? Shit. I throw the food away and slide, overwhelmed, into a puddle in the corner of the kitchen.

Before long, the door slams. Sean is home from work for lunch. "What's up?" he asks as he offers a hand and helps me to my feet.

"I think I took too much medicine. I don't remember how much. I can't remember what the doctor said, Sean. And I have an appointment with a therapist in an hour and I don't think I can drive there and I'm such a mess." I can't stop the tears from rising.

"I can take you."

"What about work?"

"I'll just take the rest of the day off. No big deal."

I release a deep breath I didn't realize I was holding and gratefully accept his help.

"I'm tired, Sean." I confess. "I'm just so tired."

In the psychologist's office, I haven't improved. I feel listless and lame and lost. She asks general questions about my childhood and my husband and then sets up another appointment for next week. It has not been satisfying at all, this day of doctors.

Two days later, dusk is falling in my mind and heart as I stumble beneath the unbearable weight of responsibility and confusion. Tonight, in bed, alone with reality, silent darkness settles on me, sticky and sickening, and I simmer in it for an unbearable hour. My heart, my blood, my mind, on fire. I've never felt anything as physically and emotionally painful as this energy charging through me. I must stop this somehow.

Even though it's 2:30 a.m., Thom picks up on the first ring. His words are thick with sleep, and then concern, when he hears my voice. "What's wrong?"

"I just... I can't. I don't know what to do." I hate myself for this, even as I say the words, but I am desperate. "Maybe we can work it out? Maybe we can just live apart for a while and see how it goes. We'll just see each other sometimes – like we're dating."

Silent pause. I know him and his hesitation. He doesn't like the idea.

"We'll talk about it later," he says calmly, decisively.

I hang up angry at myself and even more miserable. He refuses, again, to compromise. What was I thinking, handing him power again in my life? He's counting on me to fail. He never believed I could make it on my own. Tears soak my pillow and my heart is empty. Energy pulses through me and I wonder vaguely if I'm having a stroke just before my mind shuts down.

5:00 a.m. Birds. Light enters through the sheer curtains. Body still burns within. In the flame. Can't move. Need help. Doctor at 11:00. Should be sooner. Can't move.

9:00 a.m. Body won't answer. Not connected. Where are the girls? They aren't here. Nothing familiar here. No dimension or meaning. Stumbling to the bathroom. Someone in the mirror, hollow and dark and dull gray. No hope for tomorrow. Tomorrow? Today. Doctor.

A shower brings me back some. Reconnected. I feel awful, though. Dead. Dying.

The doctor is a block away. A long, agonizing block to walk. Nurse takes me straight to a room. Lie down. Better.

Blood pressure. Blood still singing, still coursing, pulsing, hammering. Doctor's face above me.

"Do you have the Xanax I gave you in April?"

"Xanax?"

"Xanax. The Xanax prescription I gave you."

"Yes. In my purse."

It's in my hand now. Dumping things. Bottle of pills. I can't open this. I can't, shaking, not opening.

"Here, let me." Gentle doctor's voice. Careful. Water and pill. Then laying quietly. Overhead light out. Peace.

"You rest. I'll be back in a few minutes."

Doctor's back and I'm better. I'm okay now. It's going to be okay. He sits patiently, sympathetically, on a stool before me. His face so familiar after all these years of care. But where are these tears coming from now? And these words spilling out and out and out? My dad's anger, my mom's illness, my unfulfilling marriage. My life. Sad and serious. Now I'm used up like a dry sponge. Doctor softly asks for someone to call to come and get me.

"I have no one. No one I can think of. No one to call."

"Then I have no choice but to either admit you into the hospital or call Thom, because you're still legally married."

"No… no. I can't. I can't go back to him"

"I don't want to admit you to the hospital, Rebecca. When they get you then they have you and they can do anything they want, including force-feeding. You don't want that and you're too sick to go home alone, so who can I call?"

"Call Molly, please." I whisper. They have her number. She treats here, too.

Alone again. Quiet. Empty. Then Sean is here and the doctor is speaking with him.

"Here's some Ensure. You'll need to buy more. It will keep her alive until she can eat again. Get her somewhere quiet. She needs complete isolation and absolutely no stress. No family. No husband. Get her to take one Xanax three times a day. It will help her to talk. She needs to talk."

My veins have stopped buzzing. I can't feel my heart throbbing anymore. Feeble, but better. The Xanax is working.

"I'm sorry, Sean. They called you at work?"

"Don't worry about it."

He takes me past curious faces in the waiting room. Resting on his arm. Shuffling feet, rubber legs. Soon at his home, though, on the soft, leather couch. Molly is not here. Neither are our daughters. There are only summer sounds and the soft rustle of Sean quietly turning the pages of a magazine at my feet. Some peace at last, even if only for a while.

Suddenly, a familiar face. Crystal blue eyes. Thom balancing lightly next to me as though any movement might shatter me. He asks how I'm doing. Concern in his eyes and, maybe, fear? How I once loved those eyes and the crisp cut of his beard. He is handsome, but today his face is lined and his eyes sad. Did Sean call him?

"I'm not sure how I am," I say. "I'm just not sure right now."

I expect him to take me home, to his home, but Sean walks out with him and only Sean returns. I am grateful to rest here. I have nothing to give anymore. There is so little left of me.

Sometime, later, Lee and Molly are framed by the sun at the end of the couch. I remember now that Molly took all three girls shopping. Lee looks fuzzy and... disappointed. *Don't worry, Lee, I'll get up. I promise. I'll be fine.*

"We're leaving, Mom. Molly's driving me."

Okay, baby. That's good. Where, again? Oh, yes, the gifted and talented program. Two weeks at the university. What an honor. I really am so proud. I love you so very much. I wish I could go, but I'm very sick right now. I see your concern. In your knowing eyes. I don't want you to see the truth, though. I just need a little more time.

Trying to focus in the bright sunlight. "Lee? Do you know you have two eyes?"

Wait... what? What? Did I say that out loud?

"Thanks, Mom, I love you, too." A roll of those expressive eyes. A little sarcasm. Frustration.

Oh, Lee, I can't think and I'm not sure I can save myself. I so wanted to keep all those promises I made to you of relaxed chats and fun and freedom and… I can't do it. Life is too hard, just like my dad, and yours, always told me. They were right. So very right.

Molly and Lee go. Elizabeth and Ann with them. Sean in the kitchen to cook. I am alone with my regret. I should be with Lee. I am failing her, and Elizabeth, too. And myself. Every day I hurt them more. I can't hold onto them now. I have to let them go. They will go on. Regardless of what happens to me, they are free of my descent. I can leave now. What pleasure to float away. No worries, no responsibilities, no more disappointment. I drift from the couch and the weight of my conscience. Senses shut down one by one. Darkness comes and soon sounds are far away and action has no consequence and thought can no longer create reality. Leaving is serene and wonderfully timeless. This is the only thing in my life that has ever been easy.

Liza

Your travel through time and space is limited and lonely. You choose your way but it does not please you. You choose your illusions of safety and security and even love, yet you do not value them. They are empty to you and filled with effort and strife. You do not find joy in them because they are of your own making. You do not find life there because you think you are alone. These paths of yours lead nowhere in the end. They simply bring you back to your beginning where you continue to search for what is not there.

It need not be so. Take just one step beyond your five senses and we are there, helping to fill your world with meaning and purpose. We come from beyond paths and searching. We are not in a form you can understand with your mind, but you do not need to understand. Allow. Allow yourself to know that there is more than you can create alone. Allow us to open the way from within and you will find what you seek. Stop wandering and desiring what does not serve you.

Let it go.

Jayd

If I could, looking back now, I would ask Rebecca to stop struggling and enjoy the disintegration. That may sound crazy, but, actually, what's crazy is living without seeing, and experiencing without knowing. When you live without substance, you really don't have a lot to stand on and the life you've created can shatter like spun glass. She learned that it's very easy to pretend in relationships. But pretending isn't stable, it isn't love, and it doesn't satisfy. There is eventually a tipping point where you can no longer pretend. So she asked for help from the heavens, and then fell into a whirlpool, swirling out of control. But that's part of the letting go and the beginning of a great adventure… and part of the journey to the bridge. That's when you get to leave behind who you thought you were, and the life that did not satisfy, and discover that you are not in control and have no idea who is. But that's okay. Perfect, in fact. Because that's when the magic happens and you begin to glimpse the light of freedom.

A Sleepover in the Mental Ward

I have survived on Xanax and Ensure for four days because Molly won't let me die in peace. I get a bottle of Ensure three times a day, right on schedule. If I refuse, she threatens to feed me with a syringe. But one little can of Ensure is like sucking down a gallon of paint.

There is so little left of me that I can barely drag myself from the couch to the bathroom, or sit up for another bottle of paint and a Xanax. Molly has played a CD of ocean waves nonstop for two days and those waters are taking me home. As the waves roll out and the tide comes in, I float. Nothing else exists. I leave my tortured body. I am primal, rhythmically breathing in harmony with the soul of the universe.

Time passes, because I wake occasionally in the darkness in the gentle peace of the night, and when I open my eyes again the sun is bright and Molly is busy in the kitchen or climbing the open stairway behind the couch to the bedroom upstairs where she and Sean sleep. Sometimes, during the day, on my shaky way to the bathroom, I pass Elizabeth and Ann. I shuffle through the living room, past the kitchen and into the bathroom praying for the strength to get back to the couch.

Today is my second appointment with psychologist Dr. Lane and I haven't the energy to even shower. Ensure for breakfast. Clothing hangs from the skeleton I've become, yet I am cumbrous and thick... and pointless. I should be back to work, but I have not improved and, worse yet, feeling like we are all a burden on Sean and Molly, who have both come with me today. We sit in silence. I have nothing to contribute and the gray girl I've become fills the room with gloom. Finally, Dr. Lane recommends that I consider going away for a while where I won't be so stressed and I can get the help I need.

"There is a hospital in another town that I believe would work out well for you. It's one of the best I've seen. It isn't a mental ward like you would see in a big hospital. It's clean and quiet and well supervised. I've heard good things about it. You could have one-on-one counseling, take a little time off and ease back into things. I'm sure your insurance would cover it and I really think it could make a big difference right now."

I don't want to go into a hospital, but Dr. Lane's picture isn't so bad. Maybe I could recover faster there and stop relying on Sean and Molly. God, I can't think straight and I hate making decisions right now. Dr. Lane's the expert and I'm sure she knows what's best. Should I follow my head or my heart?

"I don't know," I hedge as I turn to my friends. "What do you think?"

They look at each other and Sean won't commit.

"Well," Molly hesitates. "It doesn't sound too bad, but it's up to you."

"I'll arrange it for you," Dr. Lane interrupts, almost with relief.

So, late this afternoon, the 24th of June, I pack a small duffle. Lee is not here but neither is Elizabeth. Where is Elizabeth? I think Molly said she took her to stay with another friend. It's been obvious that Ann has tired of the drama and of having Elizabeth always with her. She wants her parents back. It's good that I'm going to the hospital. It's good that we don't have to burden them more. But, as Molly, Sean and I take the ninety-minute drive, I am hollow inside without my girls, and sick, and scared.

I know I look fragile and I've had no solid food in over a week. It must be obvious that I need help. At the hospital, a man with a clipboard takes me into a small white room and after a short interview he says I qualify for admission, please sign here. He copies my insurance card and driver's license and then we collect Sean and Molly and take an elevator up several floors. Sean carries the bag that contains the few items I might need as we walk a short distance down an empty hallway and through a set of metal doors with no windows. The doors slam shut behind us. An eerie energy drifts from rooms lining the long hallway running to our left and equally to our right. The very air is bleak and metallic and hopeless. A man sits limply and unseeing in a chair just to the right of a counter directly in front of us. Another person with dirty hair and a loud voice shouts into a pay phone on the wall to our right. In an instant, my temples pulse and my stomach tenses. This is a mistake and I want out. My intention was to relieve Molly and Sean of the burden of caring for me, but I did not want to trade them for a nightmare. This place scares me. It is not what Dr. Lane described at all.

A stern older woman with a clipboard leads us to a small room, empty except for a long table lined with four chairs on each side. A large man in a white uniform joins us and takes my bag from Sean.

"You need to fill out some paperwork," the lady says.

"I've changed my mind," I tell her. "I want to leave, please."

"No," she responds crisply, "You're already admitted. Only a doctor can release you."

She motions for us to sit, takes a seat across from me and begins to explain hospital procedure. It's not necessary, though, because I'm not staying. She drones in the background while the man in white removes items from my bag and inspects each of them. With each violation of my things I unravel a little more.

"Leave my things alone," I say.

I can't stay here! Dr. Lane deceived us. This is not at all the way she described it. Desperately, I search my friends' faces for help. They know, and I know, this is wrong. Anger surges and fuels me enough to rise from my chair and state again that I do not want to stay here.

"We have ways to help you cooperate," the lady responds coldly, "We can restrain you if necessary."

The man in white stops rummaging and looks at me as I return to my chair. The woman slides her clipboard across the table and tells me to fill out a questionnaire. My ability to think logically, or to even read coherently, is still limited and I struggle with it, but I have no choice now. Then the hospital people leave and Molly and Sean and I are alone.

"Sean!" I beg, "Please tell me what to do!"

"Play the game," he tells me quietly.

Play the game. Play the game. It becomes a mantra and a prayer and a lifeline.

Soon we're taken back through the doorway and to the right, down the hallway and around the corner. The walls are white, but faded by fluorescent lighting, and our footsteps echo as we follow obediently. We're taken to a corner room and I hover next to Sean. I can't help it and I hide behind him as though they can't see me. A window overlooks a parking area and a grassy hill beyond. Two single beds sit next to each other and a stark bathroom is visible through a corner doorway. No one else is here.

Sean and Molly have to leave. There is nothing more they can do for me. I watch them walk away and then I sit in despair on the bed. I understand now why they take away everything you own at the door. Soon a pretty, young girl comes in. She is my roommate and her name is Melissa. She's friendly and chatty. I am not. She got drunk over a guy, she tells me, and threatened to kill herself. She's been here a week. Finally, when Melissa has finished, I escape to bed.

I fade with the sunset, glowing softly now through the window, and I desperately want to hug my kids once more. I've lost it all in the last three months, and now I'm trapped in a bad idea. I can't breathe in this crazy place and I have a horrid headache. They won't even give me an aspirin without a doctor's order. I ask at the desk about getting a discharge. I'm told to wait until tomorrow when the hospital psychiatrist makes his rounds.

Somehow I sleep through the night. This morning, Melissa and I breakfast together and as we leave, I notice a worker measuring the food I leave on my tray. Later, Melissa introduces me to Penny, the multiple personality, with rows of scars on her arms. There are two wild-haired men behind glass who aren't allowed to walk the halls like Terry who keeps trying to touch Melissa's hair. She says he's pesky, but not really dangerous, so don't worry if he shows up in our room.

Later, I struggle through an afternoon of observation, group therapy, and "creative movement" where I meet Luke who is incredibly good-looking but not actually inside his body, and Elvie, the self-proclaimed manic depressive, who slithers around Luke and occasionally snaps a rubber band on his wrist. I refuse to participate and return to my room, despondent and frustrated, until a psychiatrist makes his rounds at 8:30 p.m.

The doctor, when he finally arrives, seems very fatherly, and moves too slowly for my liking, but he has the key to my freedom. He lowers himself comfortably and in good humor into a chair at the end of my bed as I explain cheerily how I would rather be home and it would be better for me to be with my daughters and how we're looking forward to the future. I paste a smile on my face and he waits patiently for me to finish. Finally, pointedly, he shifts position in his chair… and I know he knows I'm working too hard at this.

"Where will you go?" he asks.

"I have friends who will take care of me. I only have to call them."

He gives me a gentle smile and his eyes squint in a gesture that is fatherly and comforting.

"I don't think this is the place for you, but you have to promise that if I let you leave, you will not harm yourself. I'm making you sign this form that says so."

He hands me his clipboard and I sign gratefully, but it does not look like my signature. Curious, but I don't care. I'm getting out of here.

As I wait at the front counter to collect my confiscated property and my integrity, I feel nearly alive again. I make the collect call at the pay phone and tears rise at the sound of Molly's voice. Our excitement is mutual when I tell her to come and get me. "We're on our way!" she says. Oh, it's good to know I'll soon be back with them! I wait restlessly near the front counter as they make the long drive in the darkness. I'm terrified something will go wrong and I'll have to stay and the wait is excruciating; but, finally, finally, they are allowed to enter and we are released into the cool night air.

Home Away From Home, Again

I wake up in my friends' sunny living room this morning. They open their home to me still. Molly says she's taking Elizabeth to another friend's house to stay for a couple days. I know it's for the best. The hospital stressed me to the edge, and I am even more frail and relying on the Xanax for comfort. I will make it up to you, Elizabeth, when I get through this. I promise.

In the afternoon, I am finally able to move from the couch and I find Sean stretched full length on Ann's trampoline in the corner of the yard. I am aware for the first time that summer has finally come, spilling grass clippings and bugs and sundrops that tingle your skin when you lie still and think about it. Sean told me earlier this spring that my mood was controlling the weather. A cold and cranky spring held back the warmth and the promise of happier days, and would not budge until now, the end of June. Maybe it's a sign of better times to come.

Sean peeks at me from beneath the arm he has draped over his eyes and beckons me to join him, so I climb onto the big black circle, being very careful not to jostle him.

"Time to talk," he states. It's not a question. I am supposed to talk. Three Xanax a day and talk, talk, talk. I'd rather not, but it's certainly better than a day in the hospital.

"I don't know what to say. It's just memories that keep coming up. It's no big deal and I don't understand why I keep thinking about it."

"Just say it." Sean prods. The screen door slams and Molly hops up on the trampoline, intentionally bouncing us and getting a little groan from Sean.

"What are you talking about?" she pokes.

"Nothing, really." I hedge.

"The doctor says talk," Sean pushes with mock gruffness. "So talk!"

Talk. Messy. Private. Dangerous. Childstuff and secret. But it's been haunting me. And it won't go away. It has partnered with the divorce to help make me miserable.

How do I explain? Can I confess that I didn't like my father as a child? A lot. He had a horrible temper and he frightened my sister, my brother and me. He hit me once, I guess. I don't remember it, but Mom told me I got a spanking with a willow switch. They couldn't take me out of the house for two weeks because of the damage. He never hit again, but he was unforgiving, unpredictable and distant, and mistakes were not tolerated.

Sitting cross-legged in the middle of the trampoline, my fists are tight and my arms wrap around me. I take a deep breath and struggle for a way to explain the memories that sneak past my depleted defenses. Sean still has his eyes covered, and Molly appears to be distracted by a bird surfing the breeze overhead. A dog barks in the distance, and that is what sends me back to the past...

"I walked to school and back alone," I say softly; and I can see it again, like a dream I had once. "...when I was four years old, in kindergarten. It was at least a half mile one way. I was so cold and scared and it seemed like there were always stray dogs following me. I was so afraid of those dogs. But Mom didn't have a car when Dad worked. And Rene' and Devon were still babies."

"My mom had health problems," I explain. I have to help them understand so they won't judge my family or me. "She was so sick that she couldn't always pay attention to us. I remember when I was in high school that I'd had a bad cold for a week and my parents didn't take me to the doctor. Both of my eardrums ruptured."

I take a breath and we listen to a mourning dove as we warm in the summer sun. It feels good, and awful, to say these things. Just these couple of old memories. And I can trust my friends to keep this to themselves. I feel guilty, though, like I'm telling secrets and I can almost feel Dad's disapproval. But I'm here and he's in Florida.

I'm happy to be silent now, the three of us peaceful in the moment. I'm not even sure Sean is still listening. Maybe he's just full of June and he's dozed off.

"And?" he says from beneath the arm resting once more over his eyes, "you were saying?"

Damn. Then I hear the dog bark again, far away in the distance, and I'm lying in my childhood bedroom once more, hiding under the covers in the darkness, angry and scared, listening to the dog yelping from the beating he was getting from Dad for barking in the night.

"Dad had a bad temper," I explain. "We didn't want to cross him. Even when we were older, teen-agers, we often crawled beneath the television to get to our rooms because blocking Dad from the TV could really make him mad. And I felt bad for Devon. He had to help work on cars in the garage and Dad would get so angry he'd throw tools and hit the car with them. Poor Devon had to duck jumper cables and wrenches. I didn't have to deal with that. I worked in the house. Mom was sick most of the time and I cooked, and Rene', Devon, and I cleaned for her. She had bad headaches that would last for days."

I have to amend this... "Dad wasn't physically mean or anything like that. It was just his anger, his attitude... the sense that you were prey when he focused his attention on you." *Like a cobra in the house.*

I was always on guard, braced for any movement, gauging his actions and reactions. I shudder in the sunlight. I have to stop talking. I have to let it go. This is for me to deal with and I don't want to remember anymore. It was long ago. Rene' and Devon are doing well and have children of their own now. They've moved on, as I thought I had. They don't need to know about all this trouble I'm having. This breaking down. I'll be better soon and I don't want to worry them. I just want to enjoy the peace of the afternoon. The girls and I are safe here. Staying with Molly and Sean for a few days creates a nice, warm, summer daydream where I can relax and not worry. In the peace of the day and the lull of the medication, I can believe in the future.

But later, in the night, alone in the darkness, the truth overpowers my optimism. What was I thinking today, releasing secrets from the past? Secrets that were to remain hidden and unclaimed and better left alone? Tonight, the Xanax does not ease my pain and I awake in the morning filled with dread and foreboding. My return from the hospital was not a magic potion as I had hoped and I still can't eat. And as the memories rise, my body responds and rebels against the torment I have put it through. This is a whole new level of anxiety. A raw current of hopelessness and despair courses and burns through me, and, just as I have no control of the memories, I have no control over the torture of this new attack from within.

The next morning, Sean and Molly help me into their truck for my appointment with a new doctor. I will no longer see Dr. Lane. She referred me to a psychiatrist named Dr. Allen who greets me quietly. He appears to be in his early forties, about my age, and is lean and stylish in his tailored suit. He offers me a seat in a black leather chair, which I drop into gratefully. I don't worry about niceties today. I have no energy for that. My shirt drapes around me and I have no makeup or hairstyle, and my jeans hang loose around my hips, but this is the best I can do.

Dr. Allen asks about my childhood and my parents and how many siblings I have. I tell him my parents are still living and have retired to Florida, and I have a good, loving relationship with them. Although it wasn't always like that. Dad was hard on us as kids and Mom was always sick, but it's fine now. Really. Right now my problem is that I'm divorcing the only man I've ever loved and the only man I've ever been with. I'm scared and I'm too stressed to eat or sleep. Compounding the problem is that childhood memories keep sneaking up on me and I'm having occasional physical anxiety attacks. But once the divorce is over and I can move on, I'll be fine.

He wants to hear about any major events in my life, so I dutifully run through the familiar list of my grandfathers' tragic deaths, my car accident, and my aunt's murder. He asks how I feel about all I've told him. How I feel? I don't know how to respond to that. Events are not tied to emotion. That's just life. What's done is done. In my family, you don't revisit tragedy. You don't relive trauma. You deal with it, and then you bury it.

"It was just stuff that happened. Nothing can be done about it now." I say, irritated that he's not addressing the true problem, the divorce, and even more irritated that he's touching on memories that I'm trying to keep under control.

"But these are life-changing events," he says. "And it was as though you were reading them from a newspaper. One grandfather takes his life. The other dies working beneath a car. You hit a man with a car and kill him and your aunt is murdered? Your father was angry and unapproachable and your mother chronically ill. But you have no feelings about these events?" He raises one eyebrow and continues. "I have to say you are very emotionally flat-lined."

I don't know what I'm supposed to say. What does he expect? I've never seen a psychiatrist. I don't know the right procedure. My dad would be angry with me…with this weakness…this inability to keep going. This proof of my incompetence and failure.

Dr. Allen wants to see me three times a week and takes me off work for another two weeks. I am grateful that I saved sick time at work and I have this time to heal. I'll start eating again. I'll sleep better. I'm stronger than this. I'll get my life back. I have two weeks.

Liza

The dismantling of an unhappy life is a gift. But the world, which attempts to numb such important business, cannot believe that the purpose of all things is healing and love. Retreating from what hurts denies the cause and therefore the reward. There are wounds you inflict upon yourself. Pain that is not necessary. Peace and happiness lie not in denial of the struggle, but in the quiet and connection of acceptance and appreciation. Your world of competition and chaos creates its own rules and gratification, and carries you within its grasp. It is not necessary, but it is your way - until you choose otherwise. Hiding from your self-inflicted pain will not save you. Competing with an image of perfection, as it is defined in your world, will get you nothing. Seeking inner understanding is key. Get to know yourself, the Self that is not measured by the world but brings you joy and happiness within. Ask for help, even if you do not believe. Ask, even if you feel only emptiness. If you do not ask for help, you will remain trapped. If you do not believe in help, you are lost.

Jayd

The journey to the bridge begins in the past. Otherwise, the past will hold you back. You can't outrun it, erase it, or even forgive it unless you acknowledge its influence. You must go back before you can move forward. As honestly and realistically as possible, review how you got to your first desire for a glimpse of the bridge. It may not be fun, or pretty, or easy, but it's necessary. Otherwise, you just recreate what you already know and stay stuck where you are.

I don't recommend a trip to the psych ward, but it does help one to see things differently. Once again, Rebecca struggled with a lifeline, searching outside for something to save her. Looking inward seemed to lead only to more painful memories and more reasons to try to control herself. But trying to gather the remnants of an old life is not time well spent. It doesn't resolve the true problem, which is, in reality, the denial of the heart's desire. Her heart knew long before things collapsed that her life was a pretense, and, for all she had accumulated and accomplished, unsatisfying. She was not expressing her truth; and, in that, no longer creating.

She was simply reacting.

Meeting New Friends On Vacation

Two days later, and against my will, we're on vacation at Sean and Molly's cottage. It will soon be the 4th of July and fireworks already pop on the lake. I feel we're still imposing, but Sean just says "hospital" with a little grin. Still, I can't help it. They've already done so much. Lee is still at the university, but Elizabeth is back and she and Ann seem happy to be at the lake again. I hope she and I can finally relax, reconnect and renew in the peace of the little green cottage.

I try to rest as I shift between having anxiety attacks and becoming a creature I call "Depression Girl." She is the gray girl I see in the mirror who sees no color, no hope, no point. She can't conceive of a happy tomorrow or a time without pain. She doesn't care, she doesn't try, she has no consideration for the generosity of our friends. I can't get past her to be a good and grateful guest. I just keep fighting for control of myself and still feel like a burden and a failure.

Part of my therapy is to write and that is easier with the sun comforting me and the summer breeze at my back. So I write and pray for healing.

I don't know this person inside me. Like a little girl throwing temper tantrums for attention, but these tantrums feel dangerous. Sometimes a cloud of depression descends that steals all logic and reason. I have no will or choice. It is a chain that binds me to a dark place where no hope lies. When it lifts, the world moves again and colors reappear. I am embarrassed by my selfish actions, but there is no choice.

My past ripples in with the waves of the lake. One memory touches the rock wall on the shore and then another rolls in.

I wish the waves could cleanse the emotions attached to the memories.

I've lived with Sean and Molly for 10 days. They've been my hold on reality - on life. They've fed me and hugged me and even cried with me as I've shared my past with them. They've shown me the definition of love - total acceptance and giving of themselves.

It's time now to contact my parents and let them know I'm okay, even though I'm not sure I have the strength for it. I haven't spoken with them since the doctor insisted I have no family contact. Actually, they know very little about my life. They've been almost isolated since they moved to Florida three years ago. Our contact has been limited to phone calls and their yearly visits back home.

Sean takes me to a pay phone near a grocery store to make my call and I'm grateful to hear Mom's voice when she answers the phone. Any explanation I offer will be easier to give to her and she can pass it on to Dad. I keep it light as I let her know I'm having a little emotional backlash from the divorce but I'll be fine...

"You're stronger than that, young lady! You've always been a rock!"

My knees buckle and my stomach clenches. Dad has been listening on their other phone and now his voice cuts through me. It is not the voice of the grandpa my girls know, but of the man who raised me and Rene' and Devon. The man we loved and hated and feared and obeyed. I flash back to all those hours we were lined up on the couch in misery listening to that voice and willing the tears to climb back inside our eyes because he didn't like it when we cried. And he would go on and on and we would hear the ugliness of an unhappy soul forever battling a hateful world. And we were part of that world and there was no hope for us if we didn't listen to him and do what he said.

"I am not a rock, Dad. Not anymore." My voice sounds pinched and dry. I feel weak and worthless as I stumble through a few words of encouragement for him. I'll be fine. I'll get it together. Hope you're doing okay. Love you, too, Mom.

But my foundation just cracked a little more.

In the afternoon I sit by the lake, drained by my surprise encounter with Dad. Sean is to my left and Molly to my right, resting in deck chairs and sipping cold drinks. We are content with the soft breeze and the buzzing of speeding boats. There is happiness here and I feel uncharacteristically good. I jump up and make my way along the dock. The wooden planks are warm beneath my bare feet. Minnows chase each other in the shallows along the sea wall and beneath the dock. The lake is full of life. The whole world has come alive. I step into the lake, onto the soft sand, and the waves pull at my jeans. They drag in the current as I wade along the shoreline. The ripples take me back to happier days and forward to a brighter future.

When we got to the cottage, I could barely make it by myself from the car to the front door. I move only because my friends won't leave me behind. But right now I'm not me anymore – and it feels good. Maybe it's the change of scenery. Maybe it's the sun. I don't know what it is but it's very nice. Very nice. Problems fade, worry recedes and I am alive again. Hope! My god, how hope changes everything! Possibilities and potential and a future! I'm excited about life again. I am renewed!

"I'm going to write!" I call to my friends. "I'm going to write a romance novel! Why not!"

"Good for you," Sean smiles. "That's a wonderful idea."

Even sarcasm doesn't bother me right now. "No, really! I'm going to make some changes in my life! I'm going to change my name! If I write a book I need a new name. How about Velvet?"

How corny is that! It makes me laugh. I crack me up. I throw out a few other ridiculous names and I think I hear snickers, but my friends indulge my drama.

"I know! I'll be Lynn!" I call from the lake. "Call me Lynn!"

I continue to pace the stretch of shoreline between my friends and their view of the lake. I have to keep moving. The water feels wonderful. I feel wonderful. Strong and smart and vital. Life surges in my veins again and I just can't shut up about it. It's an amazing day!

"Help me with my plot, you guys! I need some characters and a story line and some really juicy sex scenes!" Molly laughs and throws out a few suggestions. This is so much fun and before long we've conjured a pretty good story. I can transport lonely, neglected women to another place and time, and I can give them something to dream about when the lights are out and their man is already snoring. I can do it! I never want this feeling to end. I am alive again and I like it!

Behind us now, the girls call for food and it's time to move into the cottage for the evening. I climb out of the lake and onto the warmth of the dock to follow my friends up the sidewalk. But… each… step… takes something away. Heavy, soggy jeans suck the fun out of me. My great ideas fade to wisps and nonsense. I don't understand. The good feelings are gone. I drag myself into dry clothes and shuffle to the couch.

Life… sucks…again.

The next morning, Sean and I take the two-hour trip from the cottage to see Dr. Allen. I hate that he has to take time from his vacation to drive me. There is no fresh air in the doctor's office, no birds singing or waves breaking or boaters playing. The doctor is in repose in his brown leather chair, observing and giving nothing in return. He emits no energy at all as I tell him about my friends and that I'm with them on vacation. I tell him about the anxiety attacks and that I still feel depressed and take the Xanax as prescribed. Thankfully, he doesn't want to give me any other medications. He says we can just continue to talk. I'm relieved and tell him I don't like taking drugs. Fifty minutes later we're on our way back to the lake. This feels like a waste of time and gas.

Molly has retrieved Lee from her program at the college and I can't believe how life has changed in only two weeks. Mine *and* hers. She's full of stories of new friends and experiences. She met a boy who helped her when Molly called to let her know I was in the hospital. She lights up when she talks about him. She is happy that I'm doing better, and, I think, happy to be back, and we hug each other tight.

The next day, the 4th of July, I rest with my eyes closed in the shade of the maple tree that stands between the lake and the cottage. I eat what I can and take Xanax to keep the anxiety attacks away. I make no effort to explore the beach or remember the plot of the stupid book I wanted to write yesterday, or even to breathe. Living is hard today.

There have been exhibits of fireworks each night this week and an occasional pop on the opposite shore when the sun is up, but this evening tops it all. Tonight the battles rage to our left and then our right as vacationers shoot off bottle rockets, Roman candles and firecrackers. So much noise and bother and energy. I wrap myself in a blanket with my knees to my chin. Elizabeth comes to share my chair and we cuddle while Sean builds a fire for marshmallows.

The next morning, Sean and I again take our trip to Dr. Allen. It's a nice day for a drive and Sean is wonderfully cheerful and supportive. Soon, though, he's riding with Depression Girl and with not even a pretense of conversation. She doesn't engage, she doesn't acknowledge, she doesn't care. Finally we arrive and as I take my normal place across from the doctor, Depression Girl sucks the very air from the room. The doctor and I observe each other for several long minutes. Then, with one energizing breath, my muscles expand and my lungs fill with possibility. I am alive again! The room overflows with my presence! Color fills the courtyard outside and an undercurrent, a vibration, reaches the dead space in my brain. I must move! I hop from the recliner and pace from the desk to the plush sofa across from it and back to the desk.

"I am Lynn," I announce. "I can tell you all about Rebecca, though, if you want to know. I've been with her almost from the beginning."

"You're not Rebecca?"

"No! Jesus! That poor girl? I wouldn't want her life. She's a mess right now as you can see. She doesn't eat. She doesn't sleep. I've come to help, though. I can tell you plenty about her."

"Like what?"

"Like whatever you want to know. You're the doctor. Ask the questions."

"I want you to say whatever you would like." The doctor is lizard-calm. "Tell me what you can."

"Oh, I can tell you everything. But now isn't the time. I'm stressing her out pretty badly at the moment. We'll chat more next time. I'll let her take it from here."

I scurry back into the recliner with relief. What the hell *was* that? My name is not Lynn!! What am I doing! I can't fall apart in front of a psychiatrist! He'll put me away. I'm trying for less attention, not more!

The doctor sits in silence and just watches for a couple minutes as I try to recover my dignity. When he finally speaks, it's in a moderated, considerate tone.

"Do you hear voices in your mind?"

I'm surprised at the question and have to think for a second. "No."

"Do you lose time? Have you ever found yourself somewhere and not remember how you got there? Does anyone ever remind you of conversations you don't remember having?"

"No, none of that."

He asks nothing more as he focuses on an area just past my left shoulder. Then he rises and leans against the front of his desk with arms crossed. So still. Controlled. Then he walks to a polished cherry cabinet, pulls out a file folder and hands me a checklist with two rows of symptoms down the center of the page. It only takes a few seconds to scan them.

"I believe you may have dissociative identity disorder," he explains. Then, quietly, moderated, he continues. "Multiple personalities. If you follow the list, you have all the symptoms, except one. You do not lose awareness. You don't lose blocks of time. I believe you are co-conscious with them."

A strain of a melody tugs faintly in the back of my mind. A few notes, something I heard on the radio on the way here, plays over and over again. I say nothing as I listen to the chords. I can't think of a thing to say. What *does* one say at this moment? He waits for me. I wait for him… waiting for me… waiting for him. Should say something, I suppose. Reaction… reaction… some kind of reaction. What now? What should I do with this? Seems like an awfully quick diagnosis… capable of explaining Lynn, though. Could it be? Nope. I wouldn't let that happen.

"Multiple personalities?" Weird to say it out loud.

"It's called dissociative identity disorder these days." His deep brown eyes explore my own pale blue ones. Brown to blue and back again. I say nothing. I sit quietly, as I always try to do. A vision flashes in my mind of Penny at the hospital. Scarred arms, haunted eyes, a life in and out of institutions. Her fear and confusion.

He's talking again. "Dissociative identity disorder is a coping mechanism that can help a person deal with trauma or abuse. Generally, it's the more intelligent mind that creates this defense. Your eventual outcome is unknown. I don't know how much it will affect your life because each case is unique. But I believe you can expect five to seven years of therapy to work through it. That's about average."

The melody turns into memories. Got to be good. Got to do it for Dad. Got to get it right. Failing again, missing the mark, stupid, weak and worthless.

No! Stop!! Then something else. Anger rises with tears that just graze my lower lids before I drag them back inside. Crazy me! Well, why the hell not? Might as well be insane along with the old memories and crappy divorce. Multiple personalities. Dissociative identity disorder. Multiple fucking personalities! Seriously?!

But I show none of that as the doctor escorts me out and I follow the crumbs of my sanity back to the truck where Sean has been patiently waiting.

"What's wrong?" he wonders when I climb into the seat next to him. "Rebecca, what's wrong?"

Oh, my god. Keep breathing and maybe soon you'll wake up. The doctor can't know this already. He only just met me. He doesn't understand. And I never say fuck.

Sean glances at me as he pulls out of the parking lot and toward the highway.

"What happened in there?" he tries again.

What do I say? That my whole life just pivoted? That I may be certifiably nuts? That I may not be who I think I am? Sean's known me for 24 years and in his truck we are now strangers.

"Sean, it was awesome!"

It's Lynn. Shit. "You should have been there! He said she's got multiple personalities and she's co-conscious with us. She finally knows! This changes *everything!*"

Sean says he needs something to drink and pulls into the parking lot of the nearest fast food restaurant, but he is calm as always. He leaves us, Lynn and I, alone together in the truck while he goes inside to order. I am still myself, I realize. Without someone to talk to, "Lynn" cannot exist.

Then I feel a smug sense of ownership from within. We share the body. She does exist, just as I do, in my mind, whether she has an audience or not. But I still have my thoughts. They aren't hers. I refuse to be controlled by this behavior. I will find the strength to fight it. My girls can't know about this. No one can ever know about this. What would Thom do about the girls if he found out?

Would he try to take them from me? I hug myself for comfort. It doesn't help. I am deeply shaken by this diagnosis.

Sean can't get back fast enough for me, yet I jump when he opens the door. I pull my knees to my chest and ignore the chocolate shake he deposits for me in the cup holder.

"Sean, what am I going to do?" I'm relieved they are my words, not Lynn's.

"Nothing," he tells me. "What can you do? You'll just have to wait and see what happens."

It's not a good enough answer. Not nearly good enough.

Liza

You are not whom you think. You are a collection, a composite, a voice for All. This "journey" is not yours alone. You listen to your mind as it shares your experiences and impressions. You feel your heart as it beats with joy, shame, love and woe. You change in every moment of your time and with every breath of your body. Your soul drives you to claim life. Your Self uses you to grow and expand and create. You are an expression of something greater than you can imagine. It is no great accomplishment to state your opinions and beliefs. They are fantasies of the image you claim. If you were to know your Truth, you would glory in it. You would know Love, Life and Power. Do not judge the journey you are on.

Do not yet dare to say you know what is on the other side of the bridge.

Jayd

How can we, in truth, say we know ourselves when time, space, beliefs, traditions, judgments, assumptions and expectations are always changing? When one piece of information, which lay dormant for years, can transform all that we have known and believe ourselves to be? We think we know so much and can be so smug in our complacence, but not until you are swept off the foundation you have created do you realize how flimsy it really was. This was a time of great liberation for Rebecca, although, of course, she did not recognize it then. It was the beginning of "seeing" and "knowing" and wonder and triumph and healing. It was awesome. It was terrifying. On the other side of the bridge, looking back, I see the struggle. But without it, I would still be living as Rebecca. Empty, stuck, lost, insecure, questioning. For us, it was a glorious dysfunction, this "dissociative identity disorder."

As you seek the path to your own bridge, understand that many circumstances and experiences brought Rebecca to this point. Her situation was unique, as your own is right now. She is both the hero and the villain in her world, as are you in yours. As we all are. There is no right and wrong. And no one to blame. There are choices and consequences, and lessons, truths, understandings, and insights that cannot be possible without the contributions of family and friends who struggle with their own lives. And those people may have chosen differently if they knew they could. You have your own special story, and you're responsible for it right now with the decisions you make. Choose to see the beauty and meaning in your life.

Choose from the heart.

Confrontation

I'm wary. And scared. How can I be trusted or trust myself? I sit in solitude at the lakefront upon our return from the doctor's visit while Sean chats quietly with Molly. I expect them to end the vacation, pack up, and take us home. There is nothing I can say that will make this okay.

But I underestimate my friends. We stay. We're good, and this afternoon we rest once more beneath the maple tree between their cottage and the busy lake. An occasional firecracker pops on the far shore. Everything seems normal, just as it always has through the years. I promise them I'll get myself under control. They say nothing, just an exchange of glances. But I am determined that this will not get the best of me.

Then Lynn returns to invade my life. In and out, for the rest of the day, and always in constant motion. Sean and Molly ask questions of her, trying to understand.

"I'm not her, you know. I'm me. I've been with her almost from the beginning, but I didn't do the college stuff, or the work, or the marriage." She pins Sean with an accusing glare. "Men! They're dumb as fence posts. Not a clue. They cause a lot of trouble, you know. Oh, yeah, and her job. Stuffy office, no air, no freedom. Nope, that's not for me. And, you!" She turns all her energy toward Sean again. "You'd better pay attention to what's going on here. She'll need your help. You'd better be receptive and understanding and gentle because your influence will be important."

I can't believe what comes out of her mouth... my mouth. Energy courses through me when she comes in, and my physical weakness has no effect on her. When she leaves, I deflate like a balloon out of air. But I marvel at the response she gets from Sean and Molly. Already they act like she is real. Someone they just met who is not like me at all. Next to Lynn, I feel mousy and inhibited and timid. My friends treat me differently when she is here. How can I be two different people at the same time? How can I sustain my old life and yet be taken over by this?

I keep an eye on Lee, Elizabeth and Ann as they scoot from the lake to the cottage and back again, wrapped in beach towels and carrying plastic rafts or chairs or wiping on more sunscreen. I watch them, but I have no control when this "personality" takes over. And there are no explanations that make sense. Somehow, my mind still functions and I am myself, yet I am not.

Finally, vacation is over. It's time to return to normalcy. I convince Sean and Molly that I'm well enough to return to our apartment, so it's officially our first night back in our new life after all the recent drama. As much as we enjoyed our vacation, I sense relief in both girls and the hope that maybe we can now be a family, without the constant presence of our friends. I believe I'm keeping my issues separated from my daughters. I need to make sure they are insulated from all this insanity.

Sean and Molly reluctantly let me go home, but it is time. I can't continue to bother them and I'm determined to handle this myself. Besides, I'm scheduled to return to work in two days. I tell my friends this dissociative identity thing is all just stress-induced and I'm feeling much better. I'm sure it will all clear up when I start eating and sleeping again. It won't go on much longer.

When we get home, there is lots of mail. One piece is a document from Thom's lawyer. It says I'm incapable of taking care of the girls. It says I'm mentally ill and not able to handle my affairs; that I'm on medication and living with friends. I skim the numbered accusations and I am terrified and livid. Lee scans the pages with me and her face hardens in defiance.

"What's going to happen, Mom? I won't live with him! He can't make me!"

I agree. He can't do this! He knows the girls are my life. Court-ordered visitation began in April. It was to be every other weekend and Wednesday evenings, but visits have become much more flexible. He sees them as it fits their schedules, but he doesn't complain. I know he doesn't want physical custody and they will not choose to live with him. I will fight for my children.

"Come on, girls, we're going to see your father."

We surprise him as I burst through the door ahead of the girls and he almost sprints from the living room to meet us in the kitchen. I must look like some wounded, desperate animal. He's only seen me once the past few weeks, and I've probably dropped another five pounds, but I'm breathing fire and sear him with a glare. Tears, though. Damn it!!

"Thom! Do you want me dead? Do you want to kill me? Is that your plan?" My voice quivers now with the realization that he could have a case to get the girls, especially if he finds out about my recent diagnosis. The girls flank me, torn, I'm sure, between protectiveness and fear, and we all focus on him.

"IS IT!! Because if you take them away from me, Thom, I will not make it."

He looks stricken, confused, ashamed, scared - a marquee of emotions I've never seen cross his face. He takes the paper I still have in my hand, shaking as he reads it.

"I don't know anything about this!" he sputters. "I've never seen it!"

"Bullshit! How can you not know about it? It came from your lawyer!"

"I didn't know he was going to send it! I told him not to! He's going to hear from me! I'll fix it." He's flailing now. Desperate to make amends.

"Tomorrow!" I spit. The tears begin to flow now. "Tomorrow, Thom. Don't do this."

"I won't have *them* raise my kids!" He is angry with Sean and Molly for helping me.

"*I'm* raising our girls! They're just fine, Thom, and they don't need this either. It's hard enough as it is... on all of us." My fuel is spent. I have no more energy to confront him.

"Just call it off," I almost whisper as I turn to leave. We have to get out of here now. Just being inside this house, remembering, makes me sick to my stomach.

Back at our apartment, I can't keep the girls near enough. They are my world. He will not take them from me.

We didn't last long in the apartment on our own. I'm sorry for the girls, but the confrontation with Thom took too much out of me and the next evening we're back with Sean and Molly. I don't care what he thinks. I do what I must. And I have new demons to handle now. The apartment is not our home and I can't warm it into one. I still can't eat much and I dread the night when fear stalks me. And now I'm afraid of myself. I'm afraid Thom's concerns may be justified. I'm terrified that Lynn will come out at work. Somehow I must muster the willpower to do my job tomorrow. But I also need my kids to continue to pretend everything is okay and to please put up with my reliance on Molly and Sean for just a little longer.

I return to work, but the day is a battle. The piles of paper that accumulated while I was gone make little more sense to me now than they did three weeks ago. Only three weeks? A lifetime. A bizarre lifetime ago, but there is no room for it here. No room for it in my life at all. Tonight we stay at the apartment and I force myself to behave.

The next day is just another day spent. I am spent. But I am working and I am myself. There has been no sign of Lynn. Thom called to let me know that the papers have been withdrawn from the court. It's a relief and I'm grateful to him for that. It makes my evening with the girls much nicer. We actually have a chance to catch up and relax a little. We cuddle together and share a snack while we watch television. Elizabeth melts into the lightweight blanket covering us on the daybed. Lee takes a phone call in her room for some privacy. I stroke Elizabeth's hair, then run my finger down her forehead and over her pixie nose again and again, just like when she was a baby. I pretend interest in the program, I watch my daughter doze, and I wonder how I'll find the strength for tomorrow.

Liza

So much of your awareness of life rests in your image of yourself. Your face, your possessions, your family, your work. It is so familiar to you that you believe it defines you, and any disruption to this image you have created surprises you. But you cannot be contained within a mind or a body. You cannot be limited by the choices you have made in your life, and how you feel and act based on those choices. You believe you are at the mercy not only of what is, but of what will be. But where can you go that is not home? Where is the place where there is no All? If you believe in the presence of Power beyond sight, and that what gives you life also guides every moment of every thing, then you are well. Always. And all will be well with you. It is when you do not believe that you falter and fall. There is so little that is known to your five senses. There is so very much that lies beyond them.

Jayd

There was not the comfort then that I enjoy now. The uncertainty, the collision of old and new, the weight of change, was numbing, but it was the beginning of truth. I wish I could have told Rebecca that there must be a breaking down before rebuilding can occur. That towers come down in flames and drama and confusion, but they must come down. I think, had she known what was to come, she would have given up. There may be uncertainty in the collapse, but there is mercy, too.

Oh, rising from the ashes is a grand adventure, but first... the fall.

As The World Flips

The following Friday evening the girls and I return to the lake with Molly and Sean where Lynn shows up, strong and vocal. The torture of working the past few days has taken its toll and I have no power against her. I recede to the back of my mind, watching over my own shoulder as she bulldozes into my life. The girls know I am not myself, but I'm too physically exhausted to fight anymore and the pain of anxiety attacks has worn me down. I give up. I let it go.

"Let it happen," I tell Sean and Molly. "I obviously have no control over this. Let them come in."

And so it begins. Almost instantly, I feel a shift, but I can tell it is not Lynn. *I didn't mean it! I don't want to change into someone else! What's going to happen now? Am I making it up? Why would I do that? For attention? To avoid responsibility for my life? If I'm not making it up, where is it coming from?* Too many questions flooding in. If I don't talk, maybe I can keep this new "person" to myself. I retreat to the bedroom in the back of the cottage, but the covers over my head offer very little comfort.

On Saturday morning, I wake at dawn feeling anything but comforted. I don't know how I can face another day of uncertainty. It is a hard weight to bear. I feel alone and damaged. Ironic, really, that dissociative identity disorder comes with a side of loneliness.

From the kitchen Sean announces that he's made a delicious breakfast he knows I can't resist. Trying to nurture me with food again. I trade pajamas for a pair of jeans and a tee shirt and shuffle to the round oak table with the view of the lake. To my left in the tiny kitchen, Sean loads a steaming pancake onto a plate and joins me and Molly, who's as perky as ever. The girls have eaten and sit on the end of the dock in the gentle warmth of the rising morning sun. Sean waits expectantly, with his fork poised just above his plate, for me to take my first bite. And he waits. Finally I roll my eyes, and shove a bite into my mouth. Once my first bite is chewed and swallowed, he digs into his own breakfast with relish. I appreciate his care, but I can't even eat a quarter of that giant pancake, and he scowls at me when I put my plate on the counter.

I find an old magazine and settle into a lawn chair in the sun and Sean and Molly soon join me. The girls gather fishing poles to tempt the bluegills and sunfish that nibble toes dangling in the waves off the edge of the dock. Dragonflies wander by and a boat putters past with a big black dog sitting in the bow. It's so peaceful that soon my thoughts drift and bob like ducks in the shallows and I move to the dock, dipping my toes into the cool water, and still protected by the shade of the maple tree. Shadows of leaves mingle on the water, unaffected by my feet swirling patterns among them.

I belong here, to the lake and the moment, light as a seagull's feather drifting on the surface. A melody repeats subtly in the back of my mind, moves to the left, along with a slight pressure, and takes hold. Over and over and over, I hear the same few notes that distract me from my thoughts as my world narrows to the scalloped shadows snaking across the sand beneath the clear water. With fresh eyes, I follow the contour of the lake bed inches beneath the water and drop to my knees within it. Plain sand is a kaleidoscope of brown, tan, red, beige, black, and white as it eases between my fingers back into the lake. Water caresses me and waves nudge gently. Then I rise and wade, waist deep, along the shoreline, savoring every sensation.

Sean wades now to my left. I will not let him in. A man in a paddleboat comes too close. My hands go over my ears and I feel pain at the violation of my space. Sensation is magnified – touch, sound, colors are brighter, the breeze becomes a nuzzling breath. A dog's bark punctures like a bite. I know now that this moment belongs to someone else, a being with a mind of her own and a purpose that is bound to the eternal. There is no room inside her for my issues, or for me, yet I am there, watching and feeling. My world is too harsh for her. She craves solitude and is eased by the sound of waves and fascinated by the water and I must surrender to her exploration.

She doesn't feel the temperature of the water as she kneels in the shallows to touch and play with the treasures on the bottom. This "Water Girl" is a sigh, gentle and wispy and pastel. She knows Sean and Molly watch, and maybe the girls too, but their world means nothing to her. Sean approaches cautiously, wading near. He touches her arm gently, and she recoils. I feel a burning, bruised sensation from his touch and think it's impossible that he could have hurt her. But this Water Girl's pain is very real.

She scoots away from Sean and his irritating presence and immediately forgets him. We play obliviously near the shore in the bright afternoon and I am captured within her perfect world while we inhale the beauty that surrounds us. Then Sean is here again and says something about sunscreen.

"Don't talk," she breathes.

He touches her arm again and she jerks away, startled and irritated. She walks around the point toward a sand bar but Sean cuts her off and herds her toward the cottage. She is afraid he might touch her again, but he will not give up. Frustrated with his existence, she gives in and slaps the water between them and grudgingly leaves the lake.

Her irritation brings me nearer to the surface and back to my own senses but not enough to push her out. The screen door slams behind us as she taps into my knowledge of the cottage. She runs for the back bedroom with Sean right behind her. However, this new territory frightens her and she needs to return to the lake. But when she spins back toward the door, Sean fills the opening like a stone slab. She tells him to move, horrified at the thought of applying sunscreen. He says she can't go back to the lake without it.

"Go! Go away!" She pleads, but he won't move and she becomes frantic. I wish I could tell him to back off. He's truly hurting her somehow. I don't understand, but I feel it very strongly. I try to tell her it's okay, like talking to myself when I'm scared, but it doesn't work. We can't communicate, yet we are joined.

She retreats like a caged animal, aching for the water. Finally he's more stubborn and she weakens, like a fish gasping and drying on the shore. She agrees to stay in the shade if he will only let her return to her beloved lake. He steps aside and she slips by and out into the daylight. Back we go, out of my world and into hers where she finally calms and relaxes. Soon, though, Sean catches her running her hand along the dock next door in full sun. She's forgotten her promise to stay in the shade and she doesn't understand when he says, "You lied to me. You said you would stay out of the sun." But he does not press further.

Finally, Water Girl tires of her play and I am allowed to come back. I'm grateful to be out of the strong sun as Sean and I join Molly in the cottage. It's good to rest in the cool embrace of one of the two big old couches in the living room. But I have seen another way and for just a few minutes my problems were gone. I reel from the sensations of this "alter personality." Never have I been so acutely aware of my existence. For a while, I was alive and part of every other piece of the earth. We were one in appreciation and basking in the glory of physical sensation. Now, once again, I am morbidly obese with the weight of my cares and slogging through the minutes of my life.

We wait for the grill to heat and Molly sets the table. As I relax, I feel a different sensation come over me. I am pissed. I am hateful. I despise everything in or outside of this nasty little cottage and I especially don't like these people who think they know everything and have such a happy little life and who do they think they are anyway?

Arms folded, eyes glaring, I accusingly blurt, "Why are you being so nice?"

Molly doesn't miss a beat as she sets the table. "Sorry, but you don't scare me," she says with a smile.

Sean just cocks an eyebrow and continues to leaf through a magazine. I can't believe how well they handle this and, soon, because there is no one to fight, the moment passes and I am myself again. Molly and Sean just act as though this happens to them every day.

While Molly cleans up after lunch, Lynn greets Sean at the picnic table. She says the time has come to set things right. There is no water in my soul, she says, no tears to cry. I wonder who it is that tears would heal? Depression Girl still exists in agony, creating and despising the pain. Lynn and Depression Girl oppose each other. Water Girl and Angry Girl just spun my world around. Where am I in all this?

I listen as Lynn explains to Sean that "we" were broken apart by an explosion or shattering, in an event that occurred at the age of three or four. Emotions separated into distinct personalities – some more evolved than others. She says they're like puppies, curled up and sleeping together. As each awakens and stirs and surfaces, it wakes up another. She doesn't know how many alters there are, but she implies that there are more. They didn't come sooner because I was doing my "busywork" – going to school, working, marriage, and raising kids. They appear now because of the stress of the divorce and because I let myself get so physically jeopardized. They know their appearance creates even more stress, but they have come to give me the tools I need to get through it.

I listen to my voice, explaining things I didn't know. Is crazy normal now? Is normal crazy? As I listen, I watch with envy as a young mom walks to the end of a nearby dock with her little daughter. You have no idea, lady, how fragile your world is. Once, like you, I was sure of my life. We were a family and the dishes needed doing and evenings were routine. I took it all for granted – believing it would last forever.

Liza

Take each day and each night as they come to you. Do not wish for what is not here. Engage your hopes and your fears in this moment. Each moment in your world is of itself. You do not know its true purpose. You cannot control what you do not know. You cannot see it. This is as it should be. Your time is better spent moving among the moments of your life like a child.

Observing, not judging.

Absorbing, not arranging.

You miss much in life with your worries of the past and your predictions for the future. You take on the choices and copy the images of others. You live their dreams, you walk their paths, you watch their actions to duplicate precisely. Where are you, right now?

Jayd

If we place no limits on normalcy and shed belief in how things "should be," we open to layer upon layer of what is. Rebecca missed color, sound and sensation for many years because she was looking for routine and stability. Water Girl brought Rebecca's senses to life with her profound union with each moment. The glory of sun and water and sand. That is our true stability. The green earth and the brown that helps it grow. Blue that stimulates the intellect and draws our eyes to the heavens for hope and possibility. And the sounds of living. All easy to lose if you don't let them in.

Through this alter personality, she could reach the sky and dip into the water and feel the vibrations of the earth. Rebecca had not spent time in nature since she was a child, and her body and mind were stagnant because of it. She had forgotten how to breathe in the sights and sounds and smells of the world and how to merge with them to help her to heal. Water Girl brought wonderful gifts of physical awareness and connectedness to the glorious earth that surrounds us.

And, yet, more. Meaning, purpose, grace, divinity and generosity. The gifts of the moment that underlie the colors, scents and flavors. If you feel its depth within, you will never be without it.

The Girls Find Out

The next morning, a beautiful Sunday, Water Girl eases into the lake and again my jeans are wet to the knees. She's become more comfortable with Sean, splashing him and walking in a circle around him casting glances out of the corner of her eye. She gives him a water lily as a peace offering. Playing with minnows in the shallows, she covers her ears when a paddleboat comes through. I'm embarrassed by her obvious hiding and covering her face. I feel them looking and wondering what's wrong with me.

A little later, when she retreats and lets me rest, "someone" comes in at the picnic table. I sit confused, as reality has suddenly changed again. The cottage is foreign and I feel I am not where I should be. I am drawn to the back of the cottage and through the open door of the garage, like a ghost skimming the lawn. I feel small and unsure. Sean and Molly, and then Ann, follow me. I don't want Ann there but I have no control and Sean and Molly ignore her.

I am now a child, a toddler. Molly and Sean draw her out with simple questions, but she is hesitant and shy. I feel ridiculous and want to push past her but she fills me completely. Finally, she responds to Molly's friendliness and concern.

"When I visit my Grandma and Grandpa, I play with buttons and poker chips." These memories are mine from childhood, flowing now through her. She sighs and says sadly, "But my Grandpa is gone. He went away. I didn't want him to hurt."

Tears surface as her eyes rest upon the wall and beyond, "He was smashed, all alone."

She takes me back to a sunny spring Sunday, when I was six years old, and my beloved Grandpa was killed beneath the car he was working on in his yard. We were to have dinner there that day, but the yard is filled with people. I see something covered on a stretcher in the back of a big, black car as my uncle walks from it to our car and opens the car door next to my Mom.

"Daddy's dead," he says gently as he takes her hand. She makes a sound I have never heard before and rises from the car seat. Dad rushes to her side and catches her as she collapses into his arms. He carries her into the house, leaving Rene', Devon, and me to wait in the car. Rene' was five years old. Devon was three. Hours later, after the hearse is gone and the yard empty of men who had helped, our parents return and we go home.

As I got older, it felt that we had left Grandpa's memory where he died, just as we had when my father's father took his life the year before. We were told not to discuss such painful things so as not to upset anyone. But a part of me always remembered.

The toddler finally fades back into my past. I inhale deeply as the little girl recedes and it's difficult to make eye contact with Molly and Sean. That was a deeply personal experience and I feel violated and embarrassed. I turn on Ann.

"Promise me, Ann, that you will not tell Lee and Elizabeth what you've seen! They don't need to know about it!"

She nods, but she heard it all. She knows it wasn't me. Then, in seconds, Ann bails out of the garage. I hide my face in my hands, trying to shake the memories and the discomfort. There is no way Ann can keep this to herself.

"I played with poker chips, too." Sean says. "At my grandmother's house." It's his attempt to ease the moment, but the moment carries on anyway. I take my memories into the cottage, and the long-buried feelings that return to be heard, at last, in the voice, and through the eyes, of the little girl who lived them.

After the busy weekend, I'm ready for my visit with Dr. Allen. It's been two weeks since the first "alter," as they call themselves. I've seen the doctor three times a week. Today I tell him how my friends help, and he says I'm lucky to have that. He asks about work and about my daughters. I tell him I'm trying to contain these "personalities," and so far they only talk to Sean and Molly so it hasn't affected the girls or my co-workers. He repeats that he doesn't feel medication would help in my case and that talking is the best therapy. I say I'm still exhausted and not really improving much. Those damned childhood memories still challenge me, and I never know when "someone new" will show up. I spend as much time as I can at our apartment, but most evenings we're with Molly and Sean. Thankfully, I can still work since the personalities only come in the evening and on weekends. After the session, he sends me on my way with nothing new to offer.

We're back with Sean and Molly for the night and the girls are up late talking in Ann's room. I was asleep in the living room and wake up thinking "goddamn kids!" But these are not my thoughts. These thoughts belong to a male personality who surfaces within me without notice and without my influence. He stalks to Ann's room and flings open the door to face sudden silence and three pairs of wide eyes.

"Would you be quiet?! I'm trying to sleep!" He barks and slams the door before heading back to the living room. I'm not happy with this. I am never this harsh with them. There is no reason to treat the girls this way. I have no idea what his problem is or why he's surfaced now. But over the next couple days, he rises again and says his name is Scott. I sense a young man in his early 20's. A man who is not comfortable at all in my body. That makes me happy.

Good! I attempt to communicate. *You're rude anyway. Just go away then.*

"I'm here for a reason!" This message, of course, is for me, but he speaks to Molly. "She has to remember the accident and I'm here to take her back to that night."

I don't want to revisit the accident! But instantly I'm transported again to the past. It was one week before my 22nd birthday. I leave my job just as it's getting dark and turn onto the road to my parents' house where I live. It's normally an easy 20-minute drive, but there has been road construction the past few weeks.

Ahead, warning me to move into the left lane, are two bright yellow blinking construction arrows. And there are cars pulling out of a parking lot to my right. It's not usually this busy. As I merge left, into the passing lane, trying to keep an eye on everything, there is a small explosion on the left front side of my car. I have hit something. My windshield shatters and the outside mirror breaks off and strikes the window to my left.

I hit the brakes and sit a second, shaken and confused. I had not seen anything ahead of me in the road. As I get out of the car to look behind it, several people already surround something on the pavement. I join the circle and see that it is an elderly man in dark brown clothes. My heart leaps and my breath catches. But I see him move and I sigh with relief. *Please be okay!* It was such a hard hit.

Then the man looks directly up into my eyes and smiles. I send him a prayer. *Please, God. Please let him be okay.*

Then I'm taken inside the building where all the cars were leaving by a kind man who tells me to call someone to help me. But it's hard to think. I can't call Mom. She can't handle this. Dad is at work and he'll be very angry. I can't deal with that right now. I'll call my work friend Sean. He lives nearby. Maybe he'll drive me home.

He doesn't hesitate when I ask him to come and in just minutes I meet him in the glare of the flashing lights of emergency vehicles. I wrap my arms around him for a moment for comfort and support as we look back toward the road. It is nearly blocked by fire trucks, police cars, the ambulance, traffic driving slowly by, and even people sitting in the grass, watching.

After a thorough questioning in the back seat of the deputy's car, we are released. The ambulance and fire trucks are gone now. The deputy is leaving for the hospital and says he will call me with an update.

"Do you want to go home?" Sean asks gently.

"Not really," I feel numb, but still cannot bring myself to go home. "I need a few minutes first."

Sean is unsettled, too. I've asked a lot of him tonight.

"How about if we go back to my house." He offers. "You can meet Molly."

"It's late. Will she be okay with that? I dragged you both out of bed when I called."

"She'll be fine with it." He is reassuring. Soothing. I've never met Molly, but I've heard many good things about her. I let him lead me to his car.

In their little townhouse, I'm distracted by both Molly and the living room. She's a tiny sprite in yellow baby doll pajamas with twinkling eyes and a huge smile. The kind of person who is comfortable in any situation. The living room is a collage of *stuff*. Artwork everywhere, and a massive stereo and record albums, and Christmas bulbs hanging from the ceiling, and a giant aquarium. Molly offers a seat on a blue denim-covered couch and hands me a little black velvet pillow to squeeze.

I don't stay long. I need to go home and wait for the sheriff's deputy to call.

Mom cries when I tell her. When Dad gets home from work, fifteen minutes later, he insists on getting my Camaro tonight and makes Devon go with him and drive it home.

When they return, Dad stays up with me waiting for the call from the deputy. In the muted light of the living room, he speaks of the day he lost his father. He says even the worst days pass and life goes on. He keeps talking, telling me other stories from his past. I understand that he's trying to help, but I need tonight to be about me, just this once, instead of him. I need to talk, but I listen as usual.

At 2:10 a.m. the phone rings.

"Are you alone?" The deputy asks.

Yes, I feel very much alone. "No," I say, "my father is here with me."

The deputy is kind. "He passed away a few minutes ago." he says softly. "He had a dislocated shoulder and other injuries. His body went into shock. A younger man might have made it, but he just wasn't strong enough."

So, Scott has come to make me relive this?! Wonderful.

"So it can stop haunting her." Scott tells Molly. "It wasn't her fault. It was dark, he was in the passing lane, he was wearing dark clothes. No charges were ever filed. It was an accident. She has seen it again now, all these years later and she can finally stop feeling guilty. She can let it go. And now, so can I."

I have felt guilty through the years, but partly because I got something good from a death I felt I had caused. That accident gave me the most important part of my life - my husband and our marriage and, above all, my daughters. It brought Thom and I together. He contacted me a week after the accident and we started dating. He felt so solid. Strong and capable and decisive. Here, I thought, was someone who could support me, protect me, love me.

Later, alone in our apartment, I'm still trying to shake off the sensations left by this last alter. The girls left an hour ago with their cousin in a new truck he wanted to show off. It's nice to have some time to myself. It's quiet. It's normal…. and then it isn't. I'm little again. And scared. My skin begins to burn with internal pressure and I have to scratch it for relief. I scratch my leg and my arm and my leg again, soon leaving dark red streaks. Harder and harder I scratch, but the burning does not ease. I frantically dial the phone while I can.

"Rebecca?" Molly asks. "What's up?"

"Nothing," I say, but my voice is small. I move to the floor, pressing myself against the daybed. Immediately Molly asks questions. "Who are you? Can you talk to me? What's your name?" But there is no answer and I cannot make this alter talk.

"Sean's on his way," Molly assures me, but those words mean nothing to this frightened and fragile wisp. I sense shadows and dark patches of anger and disapproval that haunt her, and her terror rises through my skin and my thoughts. She scratches at her arms and legs over and over until they nearly bleed, although I feel no pain when she does this. I feel only release, and comfort when she begins to rock. Back and forward she rocks and scratches. Molly keeps her on the phone while Sean drives into town. I'm relieved that he's coming, but I expect he will be angry. I left their house not even an hour ago.

Sean fills the doorway when he quietly enters through the kitchen. He walks lightly for a big man. The little girl won't look at him. He is not angry, though, at the pathetic creature that I am, crumpled and curled up on the floor, and he softly asks if she needs a hug. She barely nods and he eases onto the floor next to her. She snuggles against his side and tears surface and drop. He asks her name.

"I don't have one," she whispers.

"How about Bunny?" he offers.

"Okay," she sniffs. She feels safe with him and I'm grateful for his compassion. Through me she knows there is no danger here. This man would never hurt us. He gently takes her hand to stop the scratching and offers her one of Elizabeth's stuffed bears that I keep on the daybed.

I know my girls could walk in at any time and I desperately want to be myself when they get here, but this fluff of a little girl has powerful emotions that keep us both pinned to the floor, leaning against Sean and my daybed in the living room. Then, apparently because I'm thinking about Lee and Elizabeth, Bunny says she doesn't want "those girls" to see her. I pray she lets me take charge if they come home.

Just as Bunny begins to warm up to Sean, he rises and goes to the door. I hear soft voices and immediately Bunny's concerns don't mean shit to me. I don't want my daughters to see me this way!! Responsibility swells up in rebellion, and I want to shred myself and rip apart this nasty trick that is being played on us. Lee and Elizabeth have always, and will always, come first in my life and they do not need this. I have to be strong! I have to take care of them... and I can't even take care of me.

Horrifyingly, Bunny follows Sean to the door. She peaks around him, timid and unsure, but still stubbornly holding on. As the girls walk in, Lee's glance shifts from me to Sean. "What's wrong? What's going on?"

Bunny scurries back to the living room with Sean right behind and both girls follow. Then, tear-streaked and clutching the teddy bear, Bunny once again drops to the floor next to the daybed and returns to rocking and scratching.

Sean asks the girls to sit down, but Lee says, "No! What's going on? What's wrong with Mom?" There is an edge to her voice and her eyes begin to snap. She looks accusingly at Sean and there is no way out for him. As I go into meltdown inside, he gently tells my daughters that I am not Mom right now. That I am a scared little girl named Bunny who needs support. He says that Lynn is the name of another person I become. He explains that he and Molly and the doctor are helping me deal with these changes and that they have met several different personalities, but none have been scary or dangerous. He says my childhood was not always happy and that appears to be part of the problem. He is honest with them and says he doesn't know what will happen. We will just have to see how it goes.

I watch both girls arc around me, keeping their distance. I ache to go to them and hold them close and tell them it's going to be okay, but I am not in charge. Lee looks skeptical and confused, and I am inside myself struggling and fighting to surface. Elizabeth drops to her knees, searching my face for comfort. I want to explain, to reassure her, but there is nothing but actions and thoughts I can't control.

Lee tries to process what she's heard and seen, but tears pour out of Elizabeth and she tumbles over, hyperventilating. Shit. Sean tries to tend to Elizabeth but he's not sure what to do and I desperately need to go to her.

"Are we going to have to take you to the hospital?!" No! Not Lynn! Shut up, shut up, shut up!! The girls look at me in surprise at my swift change and tone, but at least Elizabeth begins to breathe again.

As though confirming Sean's explanation, I've switched from Bunny to Lynn. This isn't going to be good. Lynn beams a big smile, and with all the finesse of an elephant on ice, matter-of-factly blurts, "She's got multiple personalities. Get it?"

No, no, no! This is so wrong! Lynn explaining the unexplainable to MY kids! I am so pissed at not being allowed into my own body and for somehow creating this craziness and not being able to control it. And if I can't understand it, how can my daughters?

Elizabeth sniffles as the girls sit quietly for a few minutes, our relationship forever changed, I'm sure. Lynn perches confidently on the edge of the daybed now, waiting expectantly for questions, but, as minutes pass and the silence thickens, she cannot hold on and I return, exhausted and overwhelmed.

"It's true," I say, defeated now. "I didn't want you to know, but it isn't going away. It started two weeks ago and that's why we've spent so much time with Molly and Sean. I don't know why this is happening but I need you to understand. Please try to understand that I'm doing the best I can."

Sean quietly moves aside as the girls and I seek privacy on the deck just outside the living room. Elizabeth wipes away tears that still fall and Lee remains guarded.

"No matter how this looks," I say, as quietly and calmly as I am able, "and no matter how many personalities I may have, my love for you will never change. We will work this out together, but I need you. I can't make it without you. Please try to understand that it will take time and Molly and Sean are helping. I have no one else."

There is nothing more I can say now. I am spent and I have no strength to fight. And now I am not myself anymore. I am, once again, small and shy. Not Bunny, but another delicate child.

"Hi," she says shyly.

"Hi," the girls respond hesitantly and share a sideways glance with each other.

"I like you," the little girl says. "Will you talk to me?"

"Yes," Lee answers. "We'll talk to you, but why are you here?"

She sighs. "I don't know. I just am."

We sit quietly for a few minutes together, listening to crickets and trying to process everything, but the little girl doesn't leave, and Lee and Elizabeth begin to warm to this strange little part of me.

"Do you know who we are?" Lee asks gently.

"Yes. You belong to her."

"Yes. We're her daughters. Do you have something to say to her?"

I am no actress, and my daughters know it. The girls are respecting the existence of something they can't understand. They're respecting me. I could not be more proud of them than I am at this moment.

The little girl doesn't respond, so Lee teases a little to get her to answer.

"I just like to be here right now," the alter says. "Will you be my friends if I come back?"

"We will," Lee says. It breaks my heart.

With nothing to hold her here, I'm allowed to surface once more and I have had enough. I'm not sure how much more I could handle tonight. I grab each of the girls and hold them tight.

"I don't know what will happen next," I tell them, "but I don't want you to be afraid of me."

61

"We knew something was going on, Mom." Lee tells me. "How could we have missed it? But we'll be here for you. We love you."

Relief nearly takes me to my knees as they give me bedtime kisses and hugs as usual, tell Sean goodnight and go inside to their rooms. They are amazing. My daughters give me hope and love. It is a wonderful gift after the strain of the evening. And, silently, Sean leaves me with it.

Liza

There are many ways to find the bridge, and many who can help you. Frequently we beckon you to come to the bridge for awareness and meaning. But you do not wish to leave your dreams and your memories. You do not wish to remove what has defined you. But the bridge is your answer and your destiny. What lies on the other side, should you cross to it, is beyond your sight. But it is real, more real than the creations of your mind, and stronger than the fleeting thoughts that bind you to your world. We wait. We will always wait for you to see.

Jayd

Maybe it would have been better to have told the girls in the beginning, but a mother's desire to protect is powerful. Rebecca wanted desperately to get back to "normal," but you can't go back to what doesn't exist, and you cannot long deny the truth of what is. She stayed in an unhappy relationship for a very long time because, she told herself, it provided stability for her children. But that wasn't the truth. She wanted to protect herself. From herself. To protect the image and the problem. But being on the other side of lies, and living in integrity, is so much better.

Lee and Elizabeth, as the years have passed, have often commented on how this experience affected them. They are strong, resilient, open-minded, compassionate and sensitive because of what they saw, heard and felt. Rebecca tried to protect them from all of that. But, in the end it would not have been a kindness to keep them from their own enlightenment.

You can't learn another's lessons for them, or assume you know what's best. Sometimes you just need to get out of the way so you don't block their sun, even if you think it's going to burn them.

Sweet Surrender

It is the middle of July, my birthday, and the comforting sensation of last night is long gone. I try once again to pretend I can work, but I am weak and shaky and still look old and gray and unhealthy. I continue to sleep little and eat less. I've tried to fool everyone, especially myself, into believing I can handle all this, but I broke down in my boss's office today. She not only sent me home from work, she insisted on driving me.

I have her take me straight to Sean and Molly's and I ride in miserable, confused and exhausted silence. I can't jeopardize my job and I'm terrified of an alter coming in at work. Why can't I conquer this? I've always been the strong one in my family, the responsible firstborn. I weathered every storm with a steel spine and clear head. It's humiliating to be too sick and unstable to drive.

At Sean and Molly's house, I take a Xanax and shrink into the corner of the couch. I don't see a way out. I don't know what to do. I am broken...

And now I am someone, something, else. Formless, timeless, and genderless – wisps of something once familiar. We come to maintain the body while the essence of her snakes away, and we tell these people so. She has gone far away and may come back, but maybe not. She has thinned and hides. They try to speak with her, but there are no ears to hear, no heart to feel them...

The phone rings. It is her sister Rene', but Rebecca is not here to answer and we do not want to pretend to be her. We let her drift as she is now...letting go...releasing...giving up responsibility...

But thoughts of the girls violate my journey, and I reluctantly fall back into my body. I must return for birthday cake and ice cream and presents, and for my daughters to celebrate with me. I won't let them worry. I won't scare them. I must make the effort. And so I have a birthday, but my heart is not in it and my mind is dull.

We stay the night with our friends and Sean and Molly escort me to my morning appointment with Dr. Allen. There is no way that I can drive myself. As I settle into the soft leather chair, I wait for the doctor to speak. I have nothing to give. He asks how I would feel if he asked Lynn to talk with him. Maybe he thinks he'll get more from her than he's getting from me today.

"I guess it would be okay," I hesitate. "I don't know if it will work, though. I'm not sure about anything right now."

"Lynn," he invites firmly, "I'd like to speak with you."

He doesn't have to ask twice. Instantly, I'm out of the chair and on my feet. Pacing, taking in every detail in the office and through the window beyond... colors, shapes, sensations. She misses nothing.

"I'm here," she challenges. "What do you want?"

"I want to know what's been going on," the doctor probes. "Tell me whatever is on your mind."

"She's not doing well. She couldn't work yesterday. Her boss drove her home. Anyone could see how bad it was. She really needs to eat something. Look how these jeans are hanging on me! Yesterday was her birthday and it kind of sucked for her. She scooted right out of her body. Way out. All this is really tearing her up."

"Tell me about you, Lynn. I'd like to get to know you better."

That gets a sideways grin from her. "You'll learn all you need to know about me as you talk to her."

Damn! I was hoping to get some information myself. She's so unpredictable.

"I will tell you something, though," Lynn continues. "The alters, the others like me, have always been with her. They just didn't come out sooner because she was doing fine. She was living the life and having the kids and making it work. She was doing okay with the range of emotions she had. But now? Not so much. She's been sinking fast and taking the whole ship with her. We just can't have that, you know? The last few days have been hard on her. We've been hard on her, but it just has to be."

Lynn plops back into the black recliner and I'm almost sweating from the exertion of keeping up with her. As soon as my butt hits the cushion, Lynn is gone. I look up at the doctor in despair and embarrassment. He could see it as a game, just a patient seeking attention. He looks serious, though, and concerned, and my appearance does speak for itself.

"You can't work this way, not with all this going on. I'm taking you off work for a while. Get the disability paperwork you need from your employer and I'll fill out the forms."

Off work? Relief… and fear. How will we survive and pay bills without my full paycheck? But I know he's right. And, thankfully, I do have disability insurance. It has to be enough.

Late in the afternoon, Water Girl comes in as I rest in the sun on the trampoline with Sean and Molly. It's the first time we've seen her away from the lake. She jumps down and walks around and around the trampoline running her finger along the edge.

"We like the pretty flowers, but not those other ones." She points to flowers growing along the edge of the yard. "They're prickly and they hurt us. Flowers have life in them. There is no water here, though. We want to go back to the water. Water is cool and always touches us. It's the only touch we like. We like fish because water always touches them. We don't like noise. We don't like bugs."

Molly jumps at the chance and asks Water Girl to walk with her down the gravel road in front of their house. Molly is very careful with her. Water Girl is a gentle soul and Molly can get information for me, but if the push is too much, Water Girl will be gone.

"Why don't you like anyone to touch you?" Molly asks.

"Touching hurts us."

"Did someone hurt you?"

A breeze rustles through and Water Girl grabs it. "We like air that touches us all over."

"Are there good and bad touches?" asks Molly.

"Mad touches hurt my legs," Water Girl explains.

"Were there other mad touches?"

Water Girl rubs her left shoulder and I absorb from her a sense of pain and disbelief, but she doesn't answer the question. As we continue down the dusty road, Water Girl blends into my thoughts and I remember something my mother confided in me years ago, as though it was a secret. Something I did not remember. She said that when I was little, Dad "went up and down" my legs with a willow switch until they were raw with welts, but when he saw what he had done he swore he would never hurt me like that again. She said we couldn't leave the house for two weeks because he didn't want anyone to see my legs. I have a flash of a vision of Dad walking toward me stripping the leaves off a willow branch and Water Girl immediately disappears, leaving a metallic taste in my mouth.

This afternoon, I finally speak with Rene'. I only tell her that I'm stressed and taking some time off. She says Dad can't understand how I can be stressed so badly that I can't work or stay in my own home. I tell her I'll be okay.

Sean and Molly have a motto for me: "pleasure good, pain bad." Molly says I don't know the difference. They think I'm confused about my feelings and that I was taught to expect pain instead of love and support. I think about that this evening as I listen to summer, lying in the hammock with frogs singing, a low plane above, and a distant motorcycle running through the gears. Both girls join me, and we snuggle together and rock the hammock gently. It's a good place to escape and try to believe in pleasant beginnings and happy endings. Pleasure good, pain bad.

Later, in the dark, early hours, from the safety of my friends' couch, I write.

> *I still can't eat or sleep much. Tired of shifting and trying to rest. Tired of thinking but no way to stop. My life is so bizarre now. I watch it unfold minute by minute.*

*Trying to work reinforced my inabilities. I'm reduced
still to survival - getting through the day with minimal
stress and maximum calories. I've learned that dealing
with what's inside can be harder and much scarier than
anything coming from outside of me.*

Sean joins me at 4:00 a.m., just as I finish writing my thoughts. I don't know what brought him downstairs, but he settles at the end of the couch and watches me in the subtle light of the reading lamp. Then he says he sees something in my eyes he doesn't like, so I show him what I just wrote. I tell him I'm frustrated. I can't find anything inside to make me want to get better and start eating again and to get on with my life, and I don't think I want to look anymore. He glances at the sliding glass doors toward the eastern sky just beginning to lighten and when he returns his gaze to me, it is dark and intense.

"I will never let you go," he says. "You may give up on yourself but I will never let go. I will do whatever it takes to help you. But why can't you see it? Why aren't you learning from these childhood memories? Being hit with a willow switch is child abuse. Nobody deserves to be whipped! Nobody deserves to be ignored and to never hear that they are loved. How would you feel if someone took a willow switch to Elizabeth or if someone left Lee sick in bed until her eardrums ruptured? Would you let a five-year-old walk a mile to kindergarten, chased by dogs, and paralyzed with fear? Rebecca, admit what they did was wrong and stop justifying it and saying it was okay! Stop telling us it was just an event that happened; that they're different people now; that they didn't know what they were doing; that everyone treated their kids like that! Just stop it! All the denial and all the old excuses don't work anymore. Listen to what you've been telling us! Look what it's done to you! Admit they were wrong! Admit that what they did was bad and it did affect your life and you should be mad about it!"

He's using all that I've shared with him against me! All those pieces of my childhood that should have remained there. He isn't supposed to take it personally. He isn't supposed to care like this. I never wanted what I told him to matter this much.

His hands are firmly on my shoulders now - to keep me on the couch because I don't want to hear this. I want to get away from here. I am not betraying my family! I already feel disloyal and guilty for everything I've said about them. I love them and they count on me! I hate Sean for this, but I can only glare at him since I'm not strong enough to struggle. Finally, he relaxes a little, but does not let go. We face each other in a stubborn deadlock. Then he sighs and pulls back.

"Rebecca, have you been telling us lies?"

"No, of course not!"

"Then you've done nothing wrong. You've told the truth. That's all. You've only told the truth."

He's right.

It's time for work and he has to go. He asks if I'm all right, and I'm not sure. I haven't turned into someone else, but it would have been less painful if I had.

When Molly comes down later, I don't tell her about my encounter with Sean. But I ask how her parents showed their love for her. She says there were hugs and kisses. They told her they loved her; they comforted her and showed her in many ways how she was special and they taught her self-respect. They valued her and therefore she valued herself. As she describes these gifts of love, I probe my memory, searching for those things for myself.

I thought my parents loved me, but hugs and kisses were rare and we never said "I love you." Where were the words of encouragement and love? The safe space?

My grandfather once walked across town, at night, through a blizzard to bring candy to me and Rene', then sat on our bed, against our parents' wishes, and ate it with us. And there is a picture of me as a baby, in his arms, wearing only dribbled circus peanut candy and a diaper, with his blue and white striped engineer cap tilted over my eye. We were both grinning like naughty kids. That's where love was, in my memories, from a man who was killed long ago. And it feels far away.

I think about Sean's words. Hurtful, helpful words. Kind, painful words. The words of a friend who cares. And then, later, Lynn's words. She says that my mind is an oasis, but in the middle of the oasis is a desert. The desert is barren of emotion and we need to fill it before I can truly feel anything connected with my past.

I was awake all last night so in the evening Sean drives me to the quiet apartment for a nap. I doze while he reads a magazine he brought along, but soon I wake with a start. It is Water Girl. Sean looks up and knows instantly it isn't me. He drops the magazine and leans forward with his elbows on his knees.

"What do you need?" He asks softly, but she doesn't speak so he settles back in his chair and waits. Finally she sits up in the daybed and turns toward him.

"To be touched," she whispers in a trembling voice.

"What? Water Girl?" he asks, leaning forward again, but she can barely repeat it.

"I need to be touched." She's obviously terrified, and shivers of adrenaline run through me. What is she doing? She can't handle physical contact.

Sean moves to the end of the daybed as far away from her as he can be.

"We must!" she whimpers. "We must!" But she's trembling, and I wonder what sort of touch she's talking about. I watch Sean's face closely, just as Water Girl is, but I cannot imagine what she's doing.

"We must, we must, we must!" she cries.

I feel the emotional struggle between them - and his confusion. Should he do as she asks? How does she expect him to touch her?

He knows I watch from within, but I'm powerless to control any part of this and he'll still have to deal with me when she leaves.

She holds out her arm and Sean slowly and gently touches her forearm lightly with his finger. She winces but does not pull back. He looks so serious that it distracts me for a moment – until I feel her pain. It rips into her and through me, yet the physical part is the easiest to bear. The emotions that ride this current are agonizing, and I am only getting a portion of it. I could not take the full hit that Water Girl is getting. Only she knows what is attached to this act.

Water Girl's eyes tear as, trembling, she holds her arm out for another stroke and Sean runs his fingers lightly over the inside of her forearm. Electricity surges through the touch once more and burns to the center of us. Jesus, this is crazy! But then Water Girl pulls away and the moment is over. She wants nothing more from him and retreats back into my mind.

Liza

The touching of the soul to the physical body is a sacred connection. It is not the body that reflects on the act. It is not the body that knows why. It is the greater mind/soul. The body is the medium through which you experience and expand your awareness of yourself. It is the guardian of the soul's desires. It holds your world intact for you. It bleeds for you. It blesses you, as well. In it, you dwell for a short time, but the lessons will stay with you forever. Your body is where the physical meets the eternal.

Jayd

Admitting to the frailty of her parents, to their mistakes and sad choices, was harder than taking the pain of self-destruction. Rebecca would have protected them, because that meant protecting herself and her beliefs and her image. She would have continued to pretend that their actions were justified just to keep peace and avoid conflict. But it was all crumbling around her and just couldn't stand up to the reality of the damage that had been done.

This was the first dawning of the idea that her mind is not located within her body, and that personality is dependent on countless factors. Experience, choices, assumptions, and perceptions all play a part in our concepts of ourselves. Rebecca was beginning to understand that she could not be contained within her own created image. But what exists within when the image breaks? What truly lies at the center? There were so many questions.

There was so much more to discover.

Guides

We stay with Sean and Molly tonight and after everyone is settled for the night, I think about the odd "entities" that showed up about a week ago. Another piece of the puzzle. They aren't like the alters. No music in my brain warns of their arrival. There is no shoving my awareness to the side and forcing their way through. They simply speak through me, subtly and patiently and soothingly, to help us understand. Lynn calls them the "Others." She only says they're not "like us" and they "live over there." We have come to call them *guides*.

Molly tries to get a name or a purpose, but they only say they're here to help and to explain. They told Molly that what I'm experiencing, and she and Sean as well, goes beyond just the three of us. They say I have resources I never dreamed of and that I've been taught lies all my life about myself and my world. I've been trapped in family tradition and cultural influence and I am now breaking free. They say the alters need to communicate because of the emotional repression of my childhood.

When Molly said she was concerned that she and Sean might do or say something wrong and make things worse, the guides told her it isn't possible. Even if we feel we miss something, it will cycle back around for us again, and again, and again, if necessary. They give me the sense that we have all the time we need and that we are definitely not alone. They make me feel hopeful and loved and are giving me a deep sense of purpose and meaning in all this craziness.

These guides say I'm building a bridge to help me cross the "river" that will flow again, along with my emotions, before we are done. In my mind now, I see a landscape, parched and stark and brown, and through it runs a dry shallow spread that once contained a river. There is no longer even a trickle, yet on the right side is the beginning of a little wooden bridge. They say that before long a great abundance of water will be flowing, but for now we must just continue to build the bridge. I must build the bridge one board at a time and have faith.

We're at the cottage for the weekend and Lynn's been in all of this warm, sunny, July afternoon. She's playing with water balloons with Ann. We play all the time here and I love watching the girls battle on the big tubes out on the lake. Molly whips them around behind the bass boat and they're getting strong and tan. Everyone feels better here, it's so healthy and healing. One night we started a pillow fight that ended with all of us squashed together on the floor between the two old couches, laughing and wheezing under a big pile of pillows. Now the occasional pillow fight helps ease the tension and uncertainty as we hammer each other with cheap shots. No one escapes and no one minds when drinks spill or lamps fall over.

I wish Lee and Elizabeth could relate to Lynn the way Ann does. But Lynn isn't me and I think they feel uncomfortable when she's here. Compared to me, Lynn is outspoken, harsh and sharp-tongued and she doesn't treat them like daughters. Ann and Lynn already have a connection that *I've* never known with Ann. Ann has always dismissed me as nice and basically harmless, but she responds enthusiastically to Lynn's outbursts and self-confidence and treats her with more respect.

This afternoon, we've got whipped cream out in the kitchen for strawberry shortcake. Ann slaps a blob of it on Lynn's nose and instantly gets a return smear down the middle of her face. The whipped cream can't cover the priceless look of surprise as Ann comes back for more. Then back and forth they go and whipped cream is everywhere until they finally tumble out the front door of the cottage. I see my girls step back in amazement as their "Mom" takes on the invincible Ann.

Ann is athletic and flexible and her older cousins have taught her basic wrestling moves. She's quick and strong and I'm small and depleted, but in a wink Lynn snatches up a beach towel and in one quick motion twists and wraps it around Ann and pins her arms to her sides. Then she easily propels Ann down the sidewalk into the lake and triumphantly underwater. Ann comes up off balance, sputtering and laughing, her brown eyes huge with disbelief. Lynn just strolls up the sidewalk and back to her dessert.

More personalities and guides are coming in. New expressions and new insights every day. Sean and Molly have learned which questions to ask and how to approach each new alter. Sometimes Sean is the audience, and sometimes Molly, but the information is for me. "Move over, Rebecca," I hear from Sean and Molly. "Move over" unlocks the door to my alters. They push and I literally feel the change. Once I relax and give in to it, then my awareness shifts and the part that is me recedes into the background where I hang out, listening but not in charge, until they are done with me.

"We need to express," my personalities say to Sean or Molly, "and we need her to hear it, and you have been chosen to help." But who is choosing? Who or what is in charge?

Later in the day, I hear music in my mind, from a distance, then louder and louder. It happens sometimes when someone new is coming in. This is someone I haven't met before because this push feels forceful and masculine and aggressive. I steal away to a bench at the back of the cottage and sit in the shadows because that's where he wants to be. He?

In just moments, Sean is next to me. "What's going on?" he nudges. "Who are you?"

"Hi! I'm Guy."

How creative, I comment sarcastically in the back of my mind, but I'm paying close attention, too.

"Remember high school, Sean?" Guy says personably, as though Sean was his best buddy. "You and Molly were only a couple grades ahead of her in school. Do you remember her?"

"No," Sean replies. "I never paid much attention to the younger kids."

"Not surprising," Guy continues. "She didn't encourage attention and kept to herself. She was expected to be strong and take life like a man. Her dad was one mean s.o.b., you know? He expected blind obedience. Work hard! Get out of bed and get to work. If he caught them sitting around, he'd find something for them to clean. I thought he was nuts. And then when a girl who sat next to her in one of her classes was killed in a car accident, and she cried when she found out, he said she was too sensitive. He said she cared too much and that he would tell her when to be happy and when to be sad. Now that's tough love right there."

Guy sits silently, shaking his head, and Sean makes a noise to encourage the conversation. I'd rather he hadn't. This promises to be humiliating. Those high school days were not happy ones for me.

"Yeah, she didn't think she was anyone the boys would look at twice. And even if they did, she'd never encourage them. She was a bit overweight, plain, quiet. Her mom taught her nothing about hairstyles and makeup. And not one date, not only through high school but college, too. She just didn't know how to try. No girl stuff for her in those days."

Guy chuckles, as I'm shriveling and slowly dying inside. Oh, my god! Stop already! I'm being gutted with the most outcast time in my life. Finally, thankfully, he is gone. I just wish he would take the memories with him.

But things did improve after high school. As I worked my way through college, I dropped the extra weight. And in the years after I married Thom, I learned how to apply make-up, and dress better, and teach my girls. Looking back at it, though, as Guy rubs it in, I remember how hard it was and how I struggled.

As I sit in the emotions and memories Guy leaves behind, I realize that I was lonely in those days. I didn't live on campus in college. I lived with my parents. I didn't meet anyone. I didn't date. Not until Thom. He had many friends and they were rude, crude, and comfortable with each other. They censored nothing and their friendships were unbreakable. I didn't know such friendships existed and I craved that for myself. Marrying Thom guaranteed my place in his world and promised liberation from the stifling life I knew. I never saw it that way, until now.

Tonight, as Sean prepares the usual Saturday night bonfire, "Lady Jenny" floats in on a fragrant peach breeze, just as the twilight sky begins to sparkle with stars and the lake is rimmed with campfires and halogen lighting. I've never felt so feminine and elegant. She is a soothing contrast to Guy.

She sits at the picnic table, but is not of these times, and does not see the lake as I see it. Her world is soft and sweet and gracious. She speaks with a refined accent reminiscent of a southern belle on a Georgia plantation. When she warmly invites the three girls to join her, they gratefully accept. None of the alters has paid much attention to them and they're surprised and happy to be included.

Lady Jenny speaks to a time of cotillions when young ladies coyly danced and flirted and received their suitors. I'm delighted as I watch the girls respond to her gentility, poise, and warmth. I swear I can hear the rustle of petticoats. Life is resplendent in Jenny's world and the girls bond there with her happily as she describes the ball.

"It's much like this lake of yours," she confides. "Beautiful lights surround the dance floor and the night is warm and romantic. There are flowers everywhere and their scent is like perfume. Gentlemen and ladies attend in their finest garments. Lee, you are beautiful. You are the belle of the ball, surrounded by many enthralled young men. Elizabeth and Ann, you, of course, are there as well, in your beautiful new gowns. I see you laughing together and teasing Lee about her many admirers."

The night is magical now, sharing Lady Jenny's vision with the girls. There would be no other way in my lifetime to experience this special moment. It's a small gift but a precious one.

I would have none of this without Molly and Sean. I'm in awe of my friends' ability to give so much to my kids and me, and yet take it all in stride. And because they handle it so well, the girls have begun to adjust and even participate.

Shit and Bad News

July has heated up. Sean and I sleep in their basement tonight where it's cooler. Everyone else is upstairs with the fans on. Sean snores softly on a mattress on the floor while I doze on the vintage blue denim couch. Then I'm shaken out of sleep by a strong nudge on the left side of my brain. I wait for it to press further, or to pass, but it hangs there, sending me off balance and nearly motion sick. I sit up and try to connect, but this is not familiar. Just as it begins to take form, I am able to reach Sean, touch his arm and wake him.

Hmmm... what is this? This place of dusk, old odors and closeness? It is not here that we belong. It is not where we must act. Leave. We must leave here. We must go now. We must find it.

I catch their thoughts, their essence. More than one of them. Oh, no, no, no! I can't control this! I rise from the couch and slink like a ninja with my back against the wall, peering around the corner toward the stairway. A hostage to this new energy.

Sean rubs his eyes and, after only about an hour of sleep, struggles to get his bearings. Then he sees me inching toward the stairway, so he jumps up and blocks the way.

What is this nuisance? This presence? This delay? It is not for us to bother.

They're surprised when they can't brush Sean out of the way as they try, again and again, to push past, becoming more determined, more intense. Dodging and blocking, shifting and lunging, quickly escalate into frustrated shoving, which Sean continues to counter.

Finally, with me winded and breathing heavily, the alter stops struggling and Sean pulls back and watches warily. This is the first time I've been truly afraid of an alter, and my continued attempts to mentally push past it are futile.

"You didn't think ssshe wasss only good, did you?" It finally hisses. "Ssshe getsss what ssshe dessssservesss."

This voice is not my own. It is deep and guttural and scratches my throat. What does it mean that I get what I deserve?

It leaps for the door, but Sean's too fast and wide-awake now. He shifts quickly and pulls me back onto my stomach against the mattress on the floor and presses his weight firmly into my back.

"It's okay now, Sean. It's me again." Sean rolls away and runs his hand over his face... and I bolt for the door again. Sean grabs my ankle and yanks me back to the mattress. I spin and pull but cannot break away. I crawl for the stairs and, again, I'm pulled backward.

Several more times the alter pretends to be me and struggles to escape, but Sean no longer believes it and so we are stuck. I'm on my stomach on the mattress with Sean's weight keeping me there, taken over by an alter that makes me feel slimy and sick.

"Ssssleep now and let usss leave. There will be no sssleep tonight if you do not releasssse usss."

"I've got all night." I've never heard Sean so coolly calm.

"Why do you want to leave so badly?" Sean asks. "It's the middle of the night. Where do you think you're going?"

"It isss not here. We musssst find it. We musssst go."

"Well, you can't leave." Sean is equally stubborn and determined.

Finally, after several quiet minutes, I know they're gone as the tension leaves my body. I am exhausted, and Sean feels the shift.

"What the hell?" Sean has no bravado left.

"I don't know, Sean. I'm so sorry! I can't believe you had to go through all that. This one was just so sticky and it wouldn't listen to me. I tried to connect, but it's different than the others. Maybe...what if we ask Lynn? Will you try?"

"It's worth a try, I guess. I don't want to go through that again. Lynn? Are you here?"

I feel her come to life within me and, after the last hour's struggle, her presence is familiar and comforting. She comes in right away, but sounds groggy even after all the exercise I've just had.

"What the fuck?!" She yawns. "It's the middle of the night!"

After Sean explains, she waves distastefully.

"Oh, them. That's Shit and Bad News."

Sean smiles in spite of himself. It would be funny to me, too, if it weren't so unsettling. I've been afraid of a dark side. I haven't wanted to see one.

"They aren't hooked to her." Lynn continues. "She's not going to get any information from them. They have a mission and they don't care what you think about it. All of us have a reason for coming in. That's how it works. But take these two seriously. They're not kidding around. They'll be trouble, for sure."

"Well, what are we supposed to do?" Sean pushes.

Lynn yawns again. "You'll just have to wait and see and figure it out. Good night."

The next morning, still shaken from last night, I'm happy it's Friday and we're going to the cottage for the weekend. Because of our adventures with this new personality, when we arrive we decide to set up the camping tent in the back yard for privacy. The girls help, but we only tell them we're giving them the cottage and we'll camp out tonight. I don't want them to have to deal with this new issue. The girls don't ask questions and are very happy to have the cottage to themselves. Then, with the girls settled inside, and hoping there will be no repeat of last night, Molly and Sean and I ease into our sleeping bags in the lamplight, fully dressed just in case.

It doesn't take long, and we've barely gotten comfortable, before I feel the change come over me. Shit and Bad News again. And, again, Sean gets no answers from them. They only say they have found "the place." And they seem very determined to get to it. They tell him they're leaving. When Sean blocks the tent door, they try to push past him. Not this again!

"I'm not letting you leave!!" Sean growls. "Wait until tomorrow and we'll go with you. It's dark outside!"

He certainly doesn't want another night like last night, but they pay no attention and shove him backward. But my 100 pounds is no match for his 200, even though they seem to think it is. Sean grabs my shoulders, spins me onto my stomach and presses me into the tent floor. Twisting like a trapped animal, hissing and snarling, I am dragged into this battle with my friends. The alters pry my arms from his grip and flail and kick. I am humiliated.

"You will not hurt her." They are smug. "We know your weaknesssss."

Sean grasps my wrists together behind me and crooks his finger through the belt loop on my jeans as an anchor, and he has control, but the alter growls and threatens and squirms. On and on they struggle and try to outlast Sean and Molly until we're all ready to throw them in the lake and be done with it.

I'm trapped in this battle of wills, afraid of what's happening to me, afraid Sean or Molly will get hurt, and afraid of what this part of me will do if it gets away. Please don't let them go! Don't let them take me out alone into the darkness.

Then, in a moment of quiet while we're catching our breath, I am struck by a vision of a little green meadow, blocked on three sides by trees and bushes. To the right, in the back, is a stand of several taller trees. They've let me see it and show me that it's where they want to go, but they won't let me come back to tell Sean, and the fight escalates again. They tell Sean he is hurting me and when he loosens his grip, they struggle harder. They pretend to be me so Sean will let them go. They pretend they need water and then try to escape instead of drinking. How much more of this can my friends take? How can our friendship withstand this?

Finally, finally, they give up my body and I return tired, sore, and embarrassed. We're exhausted and crawl uncomfortably into our sleeping bags. I tell Sean and Molly about the meadow, but they are quiet and soon Sean is snoring. The rest of the night is peaceful but I lie awake, vigilant, until the promise of daylight marks the sky and the first notes of the waking birds ease me into sleep.

The Light in the Meadow

The next day is fresh and bright and I wander down the road to try to clear my mind. It's impossible to find safe space when I carry the crazy with me. I go to the end of the short road away from the lake and past a small marina. As I turn left and follow the curved road that winds around the lake, I see the meadow. *The* meadow! I've passed it a hundred times on the way to the cottage. I turn back toward the cottage and meet Sean looking for me. The alter comes in just as Sean falls into step next to me.

"Ssshe hasss found it. Thisss isss not your concern. Ssshe will do what ssshe must do."

I'm very confused, waiting within my mind for an explanation, but Sean seems to know exactly what they want. We stop near the culvert across from the marina where half a dozen turtles sun themselves on fallen logs, and Sean pulls a small knife from his pocket. He opens it slowly, without a word, and walks over to a sapling at the edge of the water. Then he cuts a branch about two and a half feet long and hands it to me.

"It's a scrub willow," he says. The alter is satisfied. I'm surprised and still confused. What's going on? Why am I the only one who doesn't get it? The alter caresses the green wood, testing its suppleness and strength. Then, in one quick impulse from the alter, I understand and ice shoots through me. How did Sean know?

We walk a short distance in the opposite direction of the meadow while the alter continues to test the willow switch. Sean wears a grim look, and I wonder if he can really let this happen as we turn and head back. At the intersection of the paved and gravel roads that lead to the driveway of the little green cottage, the alter says we're continuing on, but that Sean should go. We wait quietly for Sean's response. Will he walk away or will the struggle continue tonight? He looks defeated, and he has already cut the switch, so with a look of pained resolve and tenderness, he turns and walks away. Shit and Bad News recede. It's me now, and they are right. I know what I must do.

As I enter the meadow, healing green surrounds me and the sun warms the skin on my bare arms. It's as I pictured it last night in the tent. I check to make sure I'm alone and there are no houses where I can be seen through the trees. I hear the purr of a boat engine in the distance, and the hum of a honey bee. I poke at the ground harmlessly with my supple green stick. I want to run, but there can be no dissociation this time. I must know. I take a few half-hearted swipes at tall weeds and watch the shorn tops fall silently. Shouldn't I feel some emotion about this? All I feel is a cold resolve to get it done.

I lift the switch high and bring it down on the tender inside of my left forearm hard enough to make my eyes water. Then again and again I make that willow switch sing and sting. Broken blood vessels instantly dimple the ripe red welts crossing each other and swelling together in long burning humps. Purple dots emerge beneath the crimson slashes. Finally, after six or seven good strokes, I drop the switch and touch a swollen line gingerly and wince as it burns like nettles beneath my fingertips. And I was just a baby when these covered the backs of my legs. I breathe deeply and know that enough has been done. There is no need for more. I sigh with relief as I turn toward the road. At least now I know.

Sean waits for me near the corner. I should have known he wouldn't go all the way back to the cottage.

"How do you feel?" he asks softly.

He isn't surprised, of course, when I show him my arm. "It hurts like fury. Look."

The inside of my arm has now turned soft red and mauve with angry streaks of swollen skin crossing in patterns, dimpled with purple. And it throbs.

"Did you get what you wanted?"

"How did you know?" I have to ask. "How did you know what to do — what they needed? What, I guess, I needed?"

"I don't know. It just made sense to me after I thought about it."

We turn into the driveway and I realize this will be hard to explain as it continues to worsen with every step. It will be a long time healing.

But how do I *feel* about it? Relief, I guess. But I don't think it's just about feeling. It's about understanding. It's about knowing how much damage a willow switching, or any beating, can do. It was enough to cause multiple personalities and enough to change my life.

And more… it's about validating and respecting a little girl who bore the pain in silence and buried the secret so deeply that it took nearly 40 years for the damage to begin to heal.

In a few minutes, I settle onto the picnic table, and then I see both of my girls looking at my arm. Their anger scorches me - and Sean - because they know he was involved, or at least didn't stop me. How can I explain to them why I have these gruesome welts crisscrossing my arm? I refuse to impose my childhood issues onto the memories they carry of their grandparents. Their grandpa is affectionate and caring, and grandma cuddles and loves them and that's the way it should be. My father, however, was hard and cold and unforgiving; my mother too lost in her own pain to bear the weight of responsibility for three children.

Sean helped me so that I can move forward. I had to know how a mere "spanking," as my mother called it, could traumatize me so much. But how can I explain this to my kids?

I simply say that I did it to myself, it had to be done, and I promise it won't happen again. They aren't happy with my explanation, but they have to accept it.

Tonight Sean, Molly and I are back in the tent. I was sleeping soundly, and suddenly I'm awake and upright. Water Girl is here, as she often comes in at night. But now that I'm awake, she quickly backs out and I look down at my arm. I run my finger gingerly over the welts because they're swollen and very painful.

And now, Shit and Bad News enter again, but different. I think they're leaving. Sean rolls over and asks me what's going on, but he quickly realizes it's not me.

"Remember thisss word – *bridge*. You mussst remember. And comfort her. Ssshe will need you." And then they are gone.

After a few quiet minutes I lay back, hoping to sleep, and then my body begins to shiver and twitch and jerk. I feel fear. I am fear. A loon's sudden mournful call terrifies me, as do all of the normal sounds of the lake at night. I shake so violently that Sean moves over and puts his arms around me. Molly nestles on the other side and they try to hold me together and help me through this. Finally, Molly goes inside for Xanax so we can all get some rest.

The next morning, without enough sleep, I wake up cranky, disconnected and restless. My arm is bruised and tender and I snap at Sean when he asks about it.

"Get in the car," he tells me. "We're going for a drive."

"Whatever," I mumble.

"You didn't tell me how you feel about all this," he begins as we back out of the driveway.

"Where are we going?" I dodge.

"Who knows?" he smiles arrogantly. He annoys me when he does this.

"So, talk to me," he orders.

"I don't feel much like it," I avoid, irritated that the summer sun is violating my gloom.

"How would you feel if someone took a willow switch to Elizabeth?" he asks as he takes us away from the lake.

"I would kill them." I say calmly. "But this is not Elizabeth. It's me and I'm doing okay."

"Oh, yeah, right, sure you are," he snorts as he pointedly takes my left hand and turns my arm over. It's even uglier than yesterday. "You can't work, you're living with your friends, you can't take care of your daughters, you can't take care of your daily business! You *hurt* yourself! You have to feel *something* about what happened!"

That really smarts but mostly because, as usual, he's hit the target. I'm living with him, taking advantage of his and Molly's generosity and feeling awful about it. I'm definitely not okay.

"I need to get back on my own," I admit. "And let you have some peace."

He rolls his eyes and gives me a disgusted grunt. "That's not my point!"

I'm uncomfortable with this little display of temper. It's rarely aimed at me and I don't like it. Then he's silent as he drives, and that's even worse. Finally, he tries again.

"Listen, if you don't face what happened, if you don't 'get it' then you're not going to benefit from it. You're not going to get better. The doctor says your emotions are flat-lined, right? Well it's time to get them back. Get it out! Talk about it so you can feel something!"

I can't stand it. "Pull over!" I command. I've had enough conversation. Sean wheels to the left, into a cemetery, and we get out and wander among the gravesites.

"How do you feel about your parents coming in August? How are you going to explain the last few weeks to them?"

"I don't know what I'll tell them. I haven't even told Rene' or Devon about it. You know that."

I'm no longer the person my sister and brother knew. How can I expect my family to understand all this? And the thought of telling my father scares me.

I wander away from Sean, but he remains only a few paces behind. He's pulled this all up though, and forced an opening through which memories and responsibility surface unbidden and uncontrolled. I have to face reality, and I've been so good at avoiding it.

Rambling thoughts enter and take me back many years. Rebecca, Rene' and Devon. Such good kids. Our parents had a bond that excluded us, so the three of us formed a little family of our own. When Mom was sick, we took care of the house and I cooked. And she was always sick with gruesome headaches. We were held hostage by those headaches and suffered with her through many surgeries and trips to Mayo Clinic and other hospitals. From her darkened bedroom, she called for pain pills; powerful narcotics that she took in high doses, usually with a small handful of aspirin or Tylenol. So many doctors, and so much medicine. Acupuncture didn't help. Neither did hypnosis or biofeedback or kinesiology. Dad grumbled about all the money spent on doctors and gas and motel rooms and time lost from work. Trapped in the situation, the three of us often felt that we were part of the problem just by being there. We were good kids, and we tried, but that never seemed to be enough. We apparently weren't good enough to make Mom well and we weren't good enough to make Dad happy.

Dad doesn't understand why I can't work. He says I just need to toughen up. After I filed for divorce, they contacted Thom and told him he would always be their son. Mom told me they feel sorry for him because he's alone and has no parents. They support him and don't understand why I left him. Where is their support of me?!

The peaceful cemetery doesn't slow the avalanche of rampant thoughts and memories. I shiver in the heat and wish I could shake the claustrophobic feeling that has come upon me. I am trapped as the bodies around us are trapped. My soul stuck in a box of impotence and worthlessness. I ponder Sean's question. What *will* I say to them? How will they feel about me? Can they love me as I am? Have they ever?

"If you could say anything," Sean asks quietly. "If you knew it would turn out well, what would you tell them?"

"In a perfect world? I would say: If you love me, if you really unconditionally love me, then you will want what's best for me.

You will want me to get better and you will want whatever it takes for me to get better..."

Then, an insight. An outrageous revelation! My legs give out and I drop to the ground. My old perspective shatters and I think I understand now. It was *them*! It wasn't me! They missed it! It wasn't that I was unlovable... it was them! They were too caught in their own misery to look for love in their children. Tears threaten... and anger! Sean lowers next to me, silently watching, feeling the shift.

"I've carried that burden all my life, Sean!" I marvel. "That they were right and I was lacking. All this time, I thought it was me! I hadn't done enough. I wasn't good enough to deserve their love. But I shouldn't have to *do* anything, or *be* anything, or achieve or accomplish anything to deserve love! I deserve it just because of who I am and because I'm here. I do deserve the love that you and Molly have given me... and Rene' and Devon... and Lee and Elizabeth. Mom and Dad never said it! 'I love you' was never spoken in our house. We weren't celebrated. We were disciplined – like pets! I want to accept love, Sean! Claim my right to it! And I want to give it back! And I am sending the burden back where it belongs, my friend, as soon as my parents come home!"

Sean listens and quietly waits for me to finish and recover. How appropriate to release this in a cemetery. I need to put my past to rest. The old lessons don't work anymore and they should be dead and buried. It was once inconceivable to condemn my parents for their choices, but, now, impossible not to. I must save myself and I have to tell the truth.

Hours after we left this morning, when the sun has passed us by, we return to the cottage. Molly and the girls are toasted brown from their day in the lake, and resting on drying towels in deck chairs. They don't question where we went. They had a good day. We're just in time for food and then we gather our things for the long ride home.

Liza

Those who inflict pain on others cry for help and attention. The desire to hurt comes from longing, fear, intolerance, and disconnection. It is a symptom that manifests when you do not love, accept and heal yourself, and when you do not acknowledge the love and guidance available to you at all times. You burn with your pain and then release it onto others. That energy can, instead, be focused within for understanding and awareness. Pain is often misused and blamed on others. Its true purpose is to light the way to your own needs and desires, and to your strength and courage. It is always a messenger.

Jayd

It takes courage to travel back into pain, memories, and damage. It takes determination and strength to go to the source. It isn't easy to look the past in the eye and then actively challenge it. But that's where beliefs are seeded and where they grow. And it's those deeply held beliefs that carry you into the future. If you don't look, they will continue to play out unconsciously in all areas of your life.

Rebecca didn't see herself as brave when she used the willow switch. She was following through on a step that made sense to her. But that act of violence against herself was a catalyst for healing. Going to the center of the pain, and receiving its gifts of understanding and validation, empowered her to begin to believe in herself again. She took the blame and the pain she was carrying within and brought it into the light where she could see it better. It could no longer hide in the shadows of the past and continue to hurt.

But, more than that, and what she didn't realize at the time, is that recognizing that Shit and Bad News had a healing purpose was her first tentative step toward accepting the situation, and maybe allowing that there was much more going on behind it all than she knew.

A Powerful Good-bye

I don't go home tonight when we return from the cottage, but Lee takes Elizabeth and Ann to our apartment for the night. It gets them away from the constant drama that swirls around us. It's not an option that I stay here tonight, considering all the activity this week. And it's peaceful and comforting to be back on their couch, which is so familiar now. I drift into sleep, hoping for a calm day tomorrow. Then, as though shaken from the inside, I startle awake. My heart pounds – I can't catch my breath. I don't want to bother Sean and Molly, but it gets worse and I can't work past it. Gasping for breath, I climb the stairs to my friends' bedroom. They pull me into bed with them to calm me, but I'm nearly hyperventilating. My hands tingle and I'm so, so cold. They cover me but then I'm claustrophobic, skin prickling, and I can't stand to be touched. Water Girl is here and downloading sensation into me like a flood.

I climb out of bed and stumble downstairs to the couch with my friends right behind me. I beg for their help. These may be Water Girl's feelings, but it's my body and I'm taking the hit. I have to do something to ease this! As I slide to the floor, Sean and Molly settle next to me on the couch and Sean whispers, "send her back over the bridge."

Somehow, his words penetrate and I instinctively obey. Instantly, I see her! I see her! We're in the warmth of a perfect day and light flows from above and all around us. Flowers of all colors bloom everywhere and the grass is more green than I have ever seen. Water Girl greets me with a warm smile and I take her hand. She is young, radiant, beautiful. Hand in hand, we turn toward a lovely little bridge. I can see only halfway across, but it's enough. We take the first few steps together, and I release her. Turning back to me with a final smile, she disappears onto the bridge and is gone.

Molly and Sean move to the floor with me, waiting. They are patient beyond belief. As we sit silently in the darkness, it all comes back to me. Dad walks toward me stripping leaves from a switch he just cut from the giant willow behind the house. Mom holds Rene's little hand on the steps of the porch, watching. The sun was shining on that day, too, and, standing there waiting for the inevitable, I tremble, confused, terrified, disbelieving. A child with nowhere to run... and then... he grabs my left shoulder to hold me while he makes that willow switch sing. After that, there is nothing. But I know now that it was that touch, my father's first touch, that caused the shattering that gave birth to my alters. There need have been nothing more than that.

Tears flow silently now. Back in this world, I am cold and empty. Sean holds out his hand and says I have only to take it – there is comfort here, but I say no, there is no comfort and there is no one who can help me. I huddle into myself and sob. Emotion has never been this intense.

Finally, Sean says, "Rebecca, we're here for you, but if you want help, you have to accept it."

I can't continue like this. I must ease the pain and take the risk. Slowly I reach for his hand. It's warm and steady and rock solid. He holds his hand still for a minute and then very gently his fingers wrap around mine. Then Molly holds out her hand, too. It's an act of pity but I do not mind. We need each other in this moment because we've been through so much together. Then Molly and I hug and she cries with me.

My friends understand this moment, this good-bye to Water Girl, yet we appreciate the protection of darkness. Time passes, our bodies complain as we sit unmoving, and it's time to let this rest. Molly gathers blankets and drags a couple pillows from the couch. We will sleep on the living room floor tonight. Sean is soon snoring, with Molly on one side and me on the other. I am sorry for what has passed and for waking them, and wonder selfishly what the morning sun will bring.

I awaken alone in such a rage that it is offended by the peace of this new day. Seething torment like I have never known. Molly and Sean are not here and even their empty house cannot contain my fury. I pull on my shoes with trembling fingers and stalk out the back door onto the wooden deck, still wearing the shorts and tee shirt I slept in. As the door slams behind me, I suck in the morning dampness and vaguely feel the sun on my face. It cannot help me today. I make my way to the rolling acres behind the house, toward the woods, where a dead tree lies on its side across my path. I grab hold with both hands and pull and break and stomp and kick and crush and soon I'm sweating and out of breath, and still unappeased.

"How much is enough, Dad?! How much is enough?! *How much?!*"

I circle the broad soggy lowland that becomes a pond in the spring. There is nothing here to help me and I swing back around to the house and into the woods next to it, working my way toward the road with passion that must consume itself. Inside the little patch of trees that parallel the long driveway, I find saplings that have died young and small and I push them over with my foot. They are the dead and neglected children.

I run out and down the gravel road, jabbering, staggering, not knowing where I am or where to go. I simply go and go until, finally, I am worn, and reason returns, and I make my way back to the house. I am calm now, but I am not the same person who slept in the early hours of this day. My arms and legs are badly scraped, and dried blood droplets decorate my skin. The punishment feels right and my pain is justified.

I sit on the porch for probably hours until I realize that Sean sits next to me.

"She's gone, Sean. Water Girl is gone."

"I know." He is gentle. He understands.

Water Girl is free.

The next afternoon, I ride with Molly and Sean to my appointment with Dr. Allen, but it is Lynn who does the talking there.

"Check out the scratches and bruises, Doc. She took on a couple trees yesterday. I think the trees won."

"Lynn?" The doctor is indulgent. "What happened?"

"Well, Doctor," Lynn's voice deepens as she mocks him. "Harrumph! Let's see now... all joking aside, I'd say she's punishing herself because she can't direct the anger and the responsibility back onto her parents. She doesn't want to hurt them and so she would rather punish herself and cause herself pain than to place blame where it belongs. I feel that at a deep level, she believes she deserves pain. She got angry, God forbid, expressed emotions she's never been allowed to express, and so she feels she must be punished."

Lynn, who has been pacing around the office, smugly drops into the leather chair, and is gone.

"It's me again, Doctor. Sorry about that."

Dr. Allen says nothing. He just leans back, settles in, and waits.

"One of the personalities is gone, I think." I tell him. "The one we called Water Girl. It was very emotional and it brought up memories. In fact, it felt as though I relived those memories."

As I explain everything to him, I finally get to the question I am most interested in.

"What do you know about the integration of personalities, Doctor? What can I expect?"

"Well, Rebecca, you'll have to tell me. It's different in every case. Sometimes the individual personalities can access each other separately and they work things out, sometimes parts integrate and come together to form a whole. We'll just have to see how it goes for you."

So, there is no textbook for personality integration. No multiple personality bible. I guess I'm not surprised. I only know how I felt and what I was shown the past few days. Water Girl left her feelings with me and went home "over the bridge."

Later, in the quiet of the evening, lying alone in the dark, I begin to see what I gained from Water Girl, and what a great emptiness she leaves behind. The gifts of insight and healing are priceless, but to truly, physically experience life as she did is incredible. I had become so desensitized that those sensations no longer registered in my world. Never again can I take these miracles for granted. These alters are forcing me to feel my life when, for all these years, I've painstakingly insulated myself. I need to honor her presence, and her gentle strength, and so I write for her.

Lessons from Water Girl:

You can touch someone's heart and soul.
Touch has personality and feelings.
A touch can break your heart.
A look can touch you.
Noise can touch you.
Water and air touch you all over.
You can touch beauty.
Everyone touches you in some way.
Touch the moment.
Touch is a language.

Liza

The bridge between here and there, between me and you, is obvious once you stop looking for it from your world's perspective. It does not physically exist there, within the elaborate illusion you create, yet it is more real than anything you own. You seek answers from problems of your own making and do not know that the way to the bridge begins within you. We do not judge this. We do not place blame or rise above you. We call to you from the bridge, and, if you answer, we come to you. It must be your choice. It must be your time and your desire. Do not expect, however, that we follow your linear rules and conformity. Do not expect that we appear in all times and ways to each of you the same. We do not. As much as you open to us, we will appear to you.

Jayd

Breaking down, breaking apart, breaking through. Loss brought gain. Pain brought healing. Contracting allowed expansion. Everything was backward. This was not what she was taught. She was taught to protect and defend, as though the whole world was her enemy and life nothing more than a battle. She learned to protect the image, the possessions, and, most of all, the heart. But the heart will not be held. It is free to hope and to hold and to listen. You shouldn't try to keep the heart from its mission of love. Love is its nature and essence. It beats with hatred only if the mind is afraid. It beats with revenge only if the mind believes in loss. It breaks when the mind believes that love can be destroyed. Let your heart expand as it was created to do and it will return your life to you.

Your heart knows the way to your bridge.

Let The Party Begin

I'm in our apartment alone. Sean and Molly took the girls two days ago to an amusement park after I convinced them I would be fine by myself. They return tonight. I promise myself to try to put more distance between us. It's the first of August and we've been wrapped in this craziness for a month. I must move on and leave this troubled time behind me. I eat now, and I sleep. The girls visit their father during the week, but every weekend they stay with me. Thom seems okay with that.

Tomorrow my parents, and my sister and her children, arrive for a family celebration and I realize how well protected I've been over the summer. On weekends at the lake I transform without judgment, and explore relationships and memories and pain. But how do I explain this to my family? They will see how I've fallen, how I've declined and lost the life I had. First the divorce, and now this dissociative identity disorder. Failure multiplied by crazy. And, if I tell them, then I'm admitting it's real and that I can never go back to who I was. And what if personalities show up? Sean and Molly will be there, but so will Thom. And I hope I don't ruin this time for the girls. It's overwhelming.

Tonight, I hide with my friends, poised on the edge of change. I've learned too much and I can't pretend anymore. My memories are distorted and my perception of my family, and myself, is now skewed. Until this summer, I would have been thrilled with everyone here, and right in the middle of it all, planning, preparing and organizing. But now, the return of my family only means more pain. How do I explain that I've changed and, because I have, they've changed, too?

Chaos and commotion protect me today with everyone together for the first time in two years. Kids all talking at once and adults deciding where to meet and where to eat. Getting acquainted again is very busy work and I hang in the background and let others plan. Mom and Dad are staying with Thom, but I have nothing to do with arrangements or accommodations. The family lets me off easy and tiptoe around my frailty. I am not myself and now they know it.

I pull Rene' aside and ask her to come to Sean and Molly's tonight. She needs to know the truth. All this energy has created a tremendous amount of activity among my alters, so I've spent as much time as possible with our friends. I need that right now. Rene' has never seen me like this, and when I see myself through her eyes, it's not good. I've avoided the mirror, but even I can't miss the sunken cheeks, the paleness, and the apprehension in my eyes. I look worn and defeated and fragile.

The wide chasm between the old life and the new is viciously obvious tonight. Rene' seems worried and nervous. I wish we could just enjoy being together again, but I'm not as strong or self-sufficient as I always believed. I'm not the cornerstone of the family. I'm just exhausted and at the mercy of the alters and totally reliant on my friends to keep me going. So, Rene', how do you like me now?

Tonight, with Sean and Molly's help, we explain what has happened this summer as best we can, and Rene' is soon in tears that quickly trigger the protective big sister in me. But, as though on cue, a personality comes out to talk to Rene'. It's a shy Little One who asks for validation by reminding us what it was like when we were growing up. The times we were in trouble over little things and Dad was angry and Mom was sick. Rene' reluctantly admits that it was hard and she didn't remember much physical affection.

"I remember once," she offers, "one time when I was little I sat on Mom's lap — and she didn't seem to mind."

Sean and Molly look at each other. Rene', of course, believes this is a perfectly appropriate memory. It's simply the way it was. She is innocent, as I was at the beginning of this summer before the past caught me. I wonder if it's kinder to leave Rene' out, or to drag her in. But I have to believe there is a greater plan and if it were not Rene's time to be involved, then Rene' would not be here. So, we forge ahead.

I can't explain, I tell her, exactly what has created this situation for me. It's a combination of divorce, depletion and sour memories, but, regardless, it's what I'm dealing with right now. She says she's here for me and will help in any way she can, and we cling together in mutual support. There's a touch of resentment from her, though, and a little scolding because she doesn't understand why I didn't tell her sooner. It's certainly not that I didn't trust her, or that I thought she would desert me. It's that I had to come to terms with it myself. And I'm still working on that.

The next afternoon we meet with Mom and Dad at our apartment and it's a little uncomfortable, but the girls help. They're thrilled to see their grandparents again, and I want them to be. But I'm grateful that Sean and Molly are kind enough to be here, just in case. We haven't seen my parents since last year and, as we hug, familiar warmth fills me. I do care about my parents, of course, and even though it will be wrenching to work through it, I hope some honest sharing will be good.

But right now, I need answers, and validation. So, while the girls catch up with Dad, I ask Mom to walk with me. We make our way the three blocks to the cemetery where it's quiet and we won't be disturbed by traffic. Ancient oaks and maples shade old tombstones, the sun eases my anxiety, and the peacefulness gives me hope. I am relieved to finally get the information I seek, so I can heal, forgive, and forget. I must know for sure that I'm not making this all up and I need Mom's memory of that day in the yard when dad cut the willow switch. I need to know what really happened – and why.

I approach her carefully, lightly pressing for information. I tell her I've had some pretty serious problems since I left Thom and I could really use some insights. I tell her that past memories have been weighing me down and making it tough.

"Do you remember when I was little and Dad hit me with the willow branch, Mom?"

"No," she says. "No, I don't remember."

"Well, you told me about it when I was younger. You said it made ugly welts all over my legs. You said you couldn't take me anywhere for two weeks because the welts showed."

"It was your Dad's fault. He did it." Her face is rigid and cold.

"But why? Do you remember what I did to deserve it? I only have sketchy memories of that day and it's important that I know. Please tell me anything you can."

"I can't," she says. "I don't remember."

She has closed our conversation and we return in silence. There will be no validation here.

Tonight I need stability, so the girls and I are with our friends. As the girls watch television, I tell Sean and Molly about my conversation today. I don't know if Mom truly doesn't remember, or if she's not willing to take any responsibility. I don't want to place blame, I just want help. No, I just want a man. A sexy man. Wait. What? A man?

I like short leather skirts and red tank tops. I wish I had a pair of spike-heeled boots to wear to the bar. Men like black boots. Men like it when you rub against them as you're passing by and, after a beer or two, things could really get interesting. What about this guy watching TV? Hmmm, not too bad...

"Oh, no, you don't!!" I scream inside. "No, you don't want a man, and you certainly don't want *that* man!"

I rise from the couch and ease toward the door.

"What's up?" Molly asks.

"I'm going out."

"Who are you? What's your name?" Molly jumps up off the couch. "Why don't you stay here and talk to us?"

"Because I'm going to the bar." To the bar?!? I hate going to bars. I'm actually kind of afraid to go to bars, and certainly would never go into one alone. Somebody help me!

"What was your name again?" Molly prods.

"Krystal."

"Well, Krystal, I don't think it's a good idea for you to leave." But Molly has no authority and Krystal grabs the car keys and my purse. The girls move protectively closer to me and I see their wide eyes and discomfort at this fully functioning personality who wants to party. *Somebody please stop her!*

The sun is setting as Krystal strides toward the car, but Sean is right behind her. At the car, she spins and turns on the sex appeal. Sex appeal? Oh, my god, where does this come from!! And Sean! Sean responds to Krystal at some primitive, lizard level I've never seen in him before. His voice is lower, his demeanor is different, he's different. What the hell? Krystal bumps a hip out and puts her hand on his chest.

"You could come with me," she coos. "We'll have a good time."

She moves nearer and backs Sean against the side of the car. A glance toward the house shows Molly's and three other heads peeking through the window. *Molly! Get out here!* But my thoughts are futile and my will is useless and Krystal just smiles and revels in her power.

"That's not a good idea," Sean finally gets out. "We need to go back inside."

"Well, I can't do that. I'll be back later." Krystal runs her hand down the front of Sean's shirt and stops just north of his belt buckle as she notices that Lee is out of the house and stalking toward the car. And she was having such a good time playing both Sean and me.

"You're not leaving," Lee orders. Her voice wavers but her resolve is solid.

"I'm just going out for a little while," Krystal laughs as she gets behind the wheel.

"Then I'm going, too!" Lee spits back, and parks herself in the passenger seat. Krystal is irritated with this punk kid messing up her plans. Lee's defiance loosens Krystal's grip, though, and I feel her weaken. They sit in stubborn silence until, finally, Krystal gives in.

"Fine!" she snorts, as she bails out of the car. Lee triumphantly follows her into the house just as car headlights shine up the driveway. It's Devon. This is a surprise to all of us, but Krystal is still not budging. *This is my brother!! Go away!* But Krystal knows very well who it is.

"Let him meet me," she decides. "Why the hell not?"

Devon comes through the door, warm and friendly as always. Then he looks around at an obviously uncomfortable situation.

"So... what's going on?" he asks.

Sean and Molly are stuck now. They have to explain dissociative identity disorder. They have to explain this situation. And they have to explain Krystal. This was not how I planned to let him know.

"Hey, I'm Krystal! Nice to meet you!"

Devon waits for the punch line, but, after a brief explanation, the girls confirm that, indeed, it is not their mom. *Welcome to our world, little brother.* But then, as quickly as she came, Krystal departs, leaving all of us feeling foolish. Devon says he didn't notice any difference between me and Krystal, and heads for the door.

Saturday morning, the day of the party, brings trepidation. Last night, after the fiasco with Devon, I called Rene' and she agreed that our parents should be told as soon as possible, and that she will be there with me when I tell them. I don't want them meeting an alter the way Devon did, but I'm thoroughly panicked - and exhilarated. No one I know has ever stood up to Dad in any way... and today I will tell him my problems are partially his fault.

Sean and Molly graciously give up their house so we can have the privacy I need. Mom, Dad, and Rene' are here. The time has come. Dad sits obediently, with Rene' on one side and Mom on the other. He's in a happy mood. I wish he would grumble as usual about something – the weather, lack of money, the state of the world. But he rests comfortably, contented and curious; so I begin at the beginning and tell them about life with Thom, and his refusal to compromise. How we stopped communicating, and understanding, until our lives together finally disintegrated into nothing.

I continue describing how, last spring, after I left him, I stopped eating and sleeping and how the stress kept me from working and sent me to a therapist. I review my two days in the hospital, why we're basically living with Sean and Molly, and... dissociative identity disorder. As calmly as possible, I tell them that a mental breakdown involves consequences over which you have no control, and provides opportunities to see life differently. I explain how my past affected the present and all twisted together to become one big beast to deal with. I tell them about how personalities have been surfacing, but helping, too. And I don't know from day to day what will happen next.

I stop pacing, brace myself, and wait for their response. Rene' looks at Dad, Dad looks perplexed, and Mom appears to be thinking about something else. No one says anything, so I continue.

"I think it was the spanking with the willow switch, Dad, that did physical and emotional damage when I was a kid, but not until this breakdown was I ever aware of it. But, Sean and Molly have been helping me and I see a psychiatrist three times a week. I couldn't tell you all this over the phone, mostly because I've been so busy with it and I didn't know what was going on myself. But I'm going to be fine and I'm working really hard to get better."

"Well," Dad says abruptly. "You know, Devon is expecting us at his house to help set up for the party. I guess we'd better get going." He and Rene' stand and he helps Mom off the couch. Then he gives Rene' a hug.

As we trail behind them to the car, Rene' shoots me a confused look and I shrug my shoulders. What else can I do? At least the burden of secrecy is gone. I have that much.

Just before he climbs into the driver's seat, Dad turns and gives me a hearty hug. I wrap my arms around him and when I release him, I don't take back any regrets or resentment. It feels okay. I make my way to Mom, who's stepped out of a hug with Rene', and I move in for mine. But she puts her arms up and backs away. She says nothing, but our eyes meet and she gives me the most fleeting of satisfied smiles as she moves around the back of the car toward the door on the other side.

"What was that?" Rene' wonders as we return to the house.

"I will never understand them." I say. "Just as they will never understand me."

At the party, I'm greeted by family, friends... and Thom. We are all polite, and Thom and I are careful with each other and tiptoe through small talk. As it always was with us. We always seemed very appropriate, happy and solid in our relationship and our lives. It wasn't the truth. Not for me.

I'm aware that others watch as Thom and I meet for the first time in weeks. They all know the divorce is pending. I don't know what he's been told about me. I'm sure he's asked, and the girls have said some things. I don't know what he thinks. He's still treated by all as one of the family, and he fills that old role much better than I am filling my new one. The whole day is unreal, and a giant confused lie. I am not who I was. Life will never be the same for me. This party is a stage where I act exactly as expected.

The next day, the party is over and we say our good-byes. It was a short, intense visit. There are the usual hugs, kisses and misty eyes as cars and vans are loaded. How much this week has disrupted our family is yet to be felt, but the pebble has hit the water. Its effects may radiate through the immediate family and spiral out into the old, comfortable, emotionally stifled, sad secrets of our former lives... or it can be denied. But I choose to believe that my parents learned that actions have consequences; Rene', outside of my shadow, can cast her own; and Devon now knows that things are not always what they seem and we can't pretend that all is well. I learned that the masks I have worn all my life don't fit anymore. And, bonus, my girls got a nice break from the craziness that has been our summer.

Liza

Your lives and minds are full, stretched with what you think you know. What do you know truly? Only that which you have experienced for yourself, and even then your senses often fail you. You must desire the solitude of peace before you can seek your bridge. You must wish to leave behind much of what you have been taught, taking with you only the desire for better. To most, leaving behind the concepts that support their created image is too painful to consider. Who would they then be? How would they then fit into the world they know? They prefer to remain with their beliefs, holding them close and being comforted by what they cannot substantiate. They don't understand the burdens they carry. They cannot see the divine nature within that is covered by many philosophies and opinions. They cannot find their own truth in the darkness. The way to the bridge will become littered with your burdens of expectation, anger, guilt, shame and fear. Let them go gladly so that you may, in your emptiness, find your bridge.

Jayd

You can't put down what you can't see that you carry. We're so riveted into our ways and teachings that even the worst behavior can seem normal. It's no wonder we become confused and lost. What is right or wrong, pain or pleasure? How can you release the dysfunction that is normal to you? Have you noticed how the layers are melting away as Rebecca is able to recognize and accept them? She couldn't see this pattern of acceptance and release yet, but she could allow for the possibility that her life, and the people in it, were not what she thought. These little steps toward independence from the mental and emotional burdens were significant, and healing.

In the beginning, when she asked for peace, she unconsciously chose the path to the bridge. She did not know then how much she would change. It would have been overwhelming.

But she could handle one step at a time.

Peter Pan

After the emotions of last week's family visit, it's wonderful to have quiet time again. We're at the lake on a beautiful August Saturday. I sit in the sun on top of the picnic table with Sean and a couple of the girls, watching boats towing skiers and tubes. And then I am not myself.

I am mischief, freckles and sun-bleached hair. I am in the mind of a young boy. He shoves me aside with no effort at all and moves toward the garage, wary of the people at the picnic table. The water does not interest him. He wants a view from above. He creeps around the garage, walks the frame of the boat trailer and leaps to the top of the fuel oil tank.

I push with my thoughts, surprised at his ability to completely disregard me, but he ignores me and jumps to the ground. He seeks adventure. I can grasp his intentions, but I cannot connect with his thoughts. He wanders away from the cottage, down the dry gravel road next to the marina and into the bushes behind a boat. He wonders if they will follow, and triumph surges when Sean and Ann walk by without finding him. But then they backtrack and catch him peeking through the leaves. He pretends they aren't there as he moves to a nearby stagnant pool with turtles. He tests its depth with a stick while Sean lobs wild grapes at his back, checking for a response. The boy turns, aggressively playful, with a bit of gravel tossed back at Sean. Finally, Sean talks him back to the cottage.

He's captivated by Sean, but caught between craving attention and safely keeping his distance from this big, calm man who questions him gently. The girls, however, are a nuisance in the background and he ignores them as he inches closer to watch Sean chop firewood for the evening bonfire. As Sean works, he throws out an occasional question.

We discover that this personality has no parents. He says he's old enough to take care of himself and no one tells him what to do. Because I not only hear, but feel his answers, I name him Peter Pan.

Finally it's lunchtime and Sean entices Peter to the picnic table with a sandwich and chips. As Peter wipes a mustard smear off his cheek with my shirtsleeve, Sean steals a chip from his plate. The boy is thrilled with the game and the attention.

After lunch, he wanders into the garage and to the back of the catamaran. He knows Sean has followed, so he crawls beneath the canopy of the catamaran. Then a white plastic ball rolls out in Sean's direction. Back it comes and is immediately returned, back and forth, harder and harder. As they play, Peter's laughter bubbles unrestrained and pure, and I realize I haven't laughed like that in many years.

Peter holds tight in my body until twilight and leaves only when I have become too exhausted to sustain him. The hours of playing have taken their toll on me.

Two days later, Peter Pan dominates my time, but still wants nothing to do with those "dumb girls," even as they chase him and pester him to play. I'm amazed that the girls don't see me, their mother, but a brash little boy who is fun to tease. How we have adapted.

In short snatches of conversation with Sean, Peter gives us glimpses of his world. He lives in a place populated with various creatures that look to him for protection. Seeing it in his mind, there are intensely green forests and the vibrations of flowers. His world shimmers with energy and color, and he knows it intimately. He's proud of his ability to keep everyone safe there and always watches over them. I'm not sure what prowls in his world, but there is no way it will take Peter by surprise. One of his friends is named Chiffon, who wears a dress the color of daffodils, but his best friend is a fairy named Flit. They play together and Flit flies near Peter's shoulder when they explore.

When we leave the cottage and return to Molly and Sean's, Peter shows up again while we're all cooling off in the basement. Because he will only acknowledge Sean, the girls soon wander upstairs. I don't know why Peter sulks when they're around, but as soon as they leave he's after Sean to play. He paces around the pool table and crawls beneath it.

"Play with me!" Peter calls, but Sean just reclines across the cushions on the denim couch and watches. Back and forth Peter goes, growing bolder in his friendship with the big, gentle man. He's beginning to enjoy himself in my world and he scares me. When Peter's here, he's powerful and determined and he won't listen to my inner urgings. I'm not allowed to surface or to influence him in any way. This means we'll be spending more time with Sean and Molly because I can't trust Peter to behave. He will only listen to Sean. Later this evening, I make a pallet for him in the upstairs loft, hoping it makes him happy enough to stay put.

Kat

My nose tickles and I smell something sweet downstairs. And I smell soap. I hear the clock ticking on the far wall across the living room. I hear my heart beat even though I'm mostly asleep. My fingers flex, my claws nearly extend and the length of me stretches luxuriously. I open one eye and focus on outlines in the darkness. I like it here in the loft. I shift to my side and stretch my right leg to its full length. Ahhh… I gaze through the wooden railings and down through the sliding glass door across the living area below that leads to freedom. My nose twitches again and I take a swipe at it with my right paw. *What the…? Ohhh no you don't! What now? I'm in trouble. I have to wake my friends! I have to get them up somehow!* Wide awake now. Forcing muscles to obey, fighting my own body, I stiffly align myself into a crawling position. One hand – one knee – one hand – one knee. I creep forward in jerks and spasms six feet, past the top of the stairs and near enough to my friends' bed that they can hear me - but the most I can manage is a low growl deep in my throat.

"Rrrrrrrrr…. Sean…. Rrrrrrr… Mol…. Rrrrrrr." I clear my throat for another attempt, but I hear one of my friends roll over and I know they're responding to my feeble call as this entity, this foreign female form, races back to the bed.

This being, apparently feline, sits smugly while first Molly, then Sean, attempt to get information. I push to break through her with everything I have. These personalities are getting stronger and I continue to lose more control. I probe with my thoughts, but there is no hooking to this cat-being. She wants nothing from me. She only wants out of the house and to be free.

Then, suddenly, I'm fully back with my friends and grateful to own my clunky, clumsy and inferior body once more. She gives one last wipe of my cheek with the back of my hand and she's gone. God, I'm so tired of this!

"I'm so sorry to wake you both again! I don't know what's going on. I... I felt like a cat! I think it's done now. I'm sorry it's so weird!"

"Well," Sean yawns. "I suppose it's no odder than the rest of it. Let's name this one Katrina. We'll call her Kat for short. I'm going back to bed."

Kat returns again as the sun goes down. She comes in so subtly that I barely feel her until she has completely taken over. And then I know things that I have never known - that the evening sings, and the twilight teems with life. The final chirps of birds and the teasing scents of the night air fill my senses. These sensations tempt Kat like catnip. Her nose twitches, her ears are like radar, her mind is intense and her desire to run is overwhelming. And Kat knows no master.

Before anyone can detect the change, Kat is through the screen door and down the driveway.

I don't run, Kat!! We are not running away!

But she races toward the cornfield that covers the corner lot just yards from the house. I hear noises in the distance behind me, and Kat turns to see everyone trailing after us. She ducks into the tall corn rows and crouches silently, barely even breathing hard. How can my body respond like this? But I'm disconnected from my body and isolated in my own mind. I'm only allowed to watch. It is infuriating.

Voices call my name as my family wanders back and forth in the road, peering into the cornfield. Elizabeth's voice is shrill with fear and I curse this cat thing. It's been particularly hard on Elizabeth, wondering if I'll ever be normal again. Sean and Molly wait in the road, knowing that entering the cornfield would be futile, but I hear in Elizabeth's voice that she doesn't think they're taking it seriously enough.

"Go get her! Find her!" Elizabeth pleads. She's nearly in tears as she continues to call and beg for me to come out, while Kat squats in silent satisfaction. They chase and she runs. She hides and they seek. My eyes follow their feet, my head cocks with their movements and my ears pick up their every breath. She's enjoying this game! But pushing against Kat is like pushing fog. It makes no difference at all.

Then footsteps come a little too near and Kat flies out of the field, into the road, and back into the field. Everyone now runs back and forth through the high stalks trying to catch up and surround her. Finally, the kids head her off and turn her back toward the house, but they have sent her too close to Sean, and he's had enough for tonight. In a quick move that shocks everyone, I'm thrown over his shoulder like a sack of flour. Kat instantly gives up but does not go away. She lies limply over Sean's broad shoulder as he strides toward home.

Sean dumps me onto the grass in the yard, surrounded by the people who love me enough to chase me. The game is over and Kat fades out, leaving me with the familiar feeling of being a huge pain in the ass. I'm exhausted as I stand up and brush grass off my butt. Then I turn... and face Elizabeth's pain head-on. I can barely stand the expression on her face. She is close to her breaking point, but as she realizes I'm not going to run, and that I'm back with her, she gives me a tight hug. Again, there is no way to explain this. No other way to comfort her and ease her fears.

The next evening, the girls pitch a tent in the yard hoping that if Kat comes in, she'll be content with staying there. We're all tucked into the small tent with our sleeping bags and pillows. Elizabeth seems a little more relaxed with this arrangement and Kat has not shown herself all day, but twilight is her siren's song. As time goes on, the sun fades to soft velvet and there is no sign of a change, so the girls go into the house for snacks and a favorite television show. Sean, Molly and I recline on a pile of blankets and wait.

A mourning dove coos and I know exactly where she roosts. Frogs sing behind the house, their symphony carried on the heavenly aroma of the little pond over the hill. The leaves on the trees lining the driveway shift with a slight breeze and I hear their sighs as they wait for the calm of the night. I must join them. I must prowl. Seeing the shift, Molly and Sean move together to block the tent door, which has been intentionally zipped. My muscles tense and prepare and I sniff the scent of earth, moss and pitch from the pines that protect the house from the road. In my mind I beg Kat to go away. Please don't let this be another Shit and Bad News! She slides to the left and then to the right, then focuses on my friends who make an effective barrier. Then, with a disgusted sniff, Kat relaxes and we sit back on our heels. She doesn't want confrontation. She pushes forward once again, just a little, but there is no game to play tonight and I come back.

The next afternoon, once again, Kat is out the door and down the road, only this time my friends aren't nearly as interested in the chase. Sean and Molly make a half-hearted attempt but soon give up and wait on the side of the road. The girls continue to run after Kat who, against all physical odds, can sprint like the wind. I shout in my mind: *No one is going to hurt you!* But it's like talking to any cat and makes no difference.

Kat spots a fencerow and leaps through weeds and field grass toward it. She is intent on climbing over, but I hear Elizabeth close behind me, pleading, sobbing for me to stop. I am somehow able to force Kat's head around so I can see what's happening to my child. Lee and Ann rest, catching their breath, in the road near the edge of the field. Molly and Sean are not much past the end of their driveway, but my Elizabeth will not give up. She is only a few yards behind me. Tears streak her face. *ENOUGH!* I scream through the silence in my head. *NO MORE OF THIS!* I strain and shove to force my way back to control of myself again, then stop for a few seconds to allow air back into my lungs and to let Elizabeth see that I'm waiting for her. As she catches up and touches me, there is enough of Kat left to sear her in a cold, impersonal glare.

117

And now there is no more begging in Elizabeth's eyes. There is only terror and panic. She does not see me. My heart melts with the pain of this. Elizabeth is no longer trusting and hopeful. God *damn* this! God damn this moment and this awareness. And God damn me for whatever evil I've gathered to us. I want my Elizabeth back, undamaged and not-knowing. But it's done and I know it's done.

I turn to Elizabeth with pathetic words of reassurance, but they are nothing now. I wrap my arms around her, trying to find my little girl in this disaster... and Elizabeth does not respond. Tears and pain warp her face and I realize that she thought I was gone. Lost to these personalities the way her father is now lost to us.

"I dddidn't think you were coming back!" she finally sobs.

"Oh, baby, I'll come back. I'll always come back to you." I wipe the tears away as I try to reassure her once more that this insanity will end. I wish someone could make me the same promise.

The next day, Friday, we return to the cottage for the last summer weekend before school starts. I'm anxious about sending the girls to school with all this chaos in their lives. It's another worry and a concern I can't control.

Elizabeth and I have a truce today and she stays close to me. We do not acknowledge what we shared in the field. My apologies have no more meaning. Words are worthless. Time and proof hold the only hope I have of renewing her trust in me.

Everyone is understandably vigilant while Kat remains the most active personality, and I wish we could just find a leash or a cage or something. Ludicrous doesn't even cover it anymore. Molly and Sean attempt to keep me safe by blocking the cottage doors so they can hear if I try to leave in the night, but Kat is relentless as she paces and stalks the fresh air and soon Molly is tired of playing. Finally, frustration and impatience get the best of Molly and she says, "I'm going to bed. Whatever happens, happens!" I'm surprised it's taken this long to get her fill.

So, in the very early morning hours, I wake up as Kat steals out of the cottage and into the cool dawn. The lake is frosted with mist that hovers in the coves and reflects in the glassy water. The first call of a bird drifts in from the trees behind the cottage and Kat turns in that direction. She pads down the gravel drive toward the paved road in a pair of white socks that I wear as slippers. Thankfully, I slept in my usual shorts and tee-shirt last night, but she did not stop to put on shoes. My nose is filled with morning smells and my mind races with a mixture of her exhilaration and my fear that someone will see me. I have no idea what she plans as she moves dangerously close to the slimy turtle pond. What a nightmare! A runaway personality, and an animal one at that! They're going to lock me up.

I'm grateful that she was simply curious about the pond and we prowl a little further down the road. Then I hear a car heading our way and Kat leaps for the undergrowth next to the road where she hunkers down and waits for it to pass. My feet are soaked and freezing, my skin covered with goose bumps, and I'm shivering, but Kat notices none of this. I press with my mind to free myself of the weight of her, but she is anchored and I am under her control.

Kat prowls the thickets at the edge of the road until, at last, as the sun climbs the east side of the lake and begins to warm the land, I stand on the side of the road alone. Kat is gone for now. *Thank you, God!!* I can't get back to the cottage fast enough. As I quietly push open the door, I find that everyone is still soundly sleeping, none the wiser of my adventure. I toss the wet, cold socks onto the floor and creep into bed, shivering and frustrated. I am trapped in this insanity, as always. I may belong in an institution, but I am terrified at the thought. I rely on the tolerance of my friends, but they can stop the game in a second.

"Go home, Rebecca," I hear them say in my head. "Go home with your craziness and your kids and your problems. Find somebody else to deal with you." My stomach churns at the thought. I must rely on them as long as they will have me.

On Sunday, Peter Pan comes in after our return from the lake. It's at least a break from Kat. He seems shy, but playful, and scoots off the couch where I was sitting and crawls to a more secure space behind some pillows across the room. Molly and the girls have gone to the store, so Sean keeps an eye on him. Sean, very aware that Peter is watching, nonchalantly and very intentionally picks up a piece of notebook paper and pretends it's the most important thing in the world. Instantly, nothing exists for Peter except that one sheet of paper. He cocks his head to the left, fascinated with what this magic might be.

Ever so slowly, Sean creates crisp, sleek wings and the sharp pointed nose of a paper airplane. Then, with just a tiny thrust into the air, it drifts in a short spiral around the room, finally resting just a couple feet to Peter's left. Adrenaline pumps through my body as Peter's joy fills us both. Soon another plane glides in and then more and more until the floor is carpeted with various styles of paper masterpieces. It's fun for me, too, as Peter's giggles melt the iciness of Kat's residue in my mind. Peter is warm and emotional and honest. Kat is heartless. She wants to get away. Peter wants to come and play.

We return to our apartment tonight because the new school year starts in the morning. Lee is a junior in high school now. She got a job earlier this summer and bought her own clothes. It helped a lot. She's blossomed this year, in spite of all the changes, and achieved maturity and independence that would have been impossible six months ago. I am truly in awe of her.

Elizabeth and Ann start 7th grade, but will not likely be in the same classes. I'm glad because they've been forced together constantly this summer. At times it strained their relationship to the edge and still they had no choice. They ate together, played together, fought, shared a bedroom and worked out their disagreements mostly on their own. It's time for them now to reconnect with other friends.

But after school we return to Sean and Molly's for the evening because the alters have been so active lately. After dinner, Ann and Elizabeth go to the basement alone and I steal down the stairs as well, unnoticed by Molly or Sean. I glide past the girls into a corner where very little light can reach. I finally realize that it is Kat, and she is very aware that only Elizabeth and Ann are here. I'm confused because she has intentionally come to see them, and never has she acknowledged them at all. She's made no attempt to communicate with them, or anyone else. Almost by some unspoken agreement, the girls come to me, to Kat, and sit cross-legged before us, silently waiting in the twilight. Then Kat speaks so softly that I wonder how the girls can hear her. She breathes her words, like warm purrs.

"It is about freedom. You must understand this." I, like the kids, hang on every word. I have to get this. I have to know, because even the guides have not been helpful with Kat. And, now, why does she seek Elizabeth and Ann?

"She does not know freedom. She was not allowed freedom, but it is important to understand. It has extremes. You must realize. Total freedom can be lonely. But no freedom is dangerous. She must understand how to share her life with others, but to also be like a cat and be free in any situation. She must learn to choose for herself. She must learn what freedom truly means." Kat smiles at the girls as they sit perfectly still, entranced. Their eyes never leave hers and I feel a connection they have not had with any of the other alters.

"Even housecats have their freedom," Kat whispers with a gentle smile. "No one ever really owns them. You must understand that running and hiding allows the chase. What is important is having someone care about you enough to chase you. Not for what you can give them when they catch you, but because of an unconditional desire to be there for you. Everyone needs to be chased. Everyone needs to be loved that much."

I see understanding in Elizabeth's eyes... and peace. She gets it. I get it. And Kat is gone.

Liza

You have created this world you choose to believe in. You have made it your altar and you worship it. This creation of yours excites, challenges, stimulates, and appeases you. It is your child and you have raised it. You can build a different world, and a new self, anytime you like.

No one lives in a perfect world. No one has all the answers. Some like rain, some the warmth of a sunny day. Who is right? Some like to fight and some to hide. Who is right? Who, on your earth, is right? Who is accountable? None of the world's rules are binding. They are only as strong as those who enforce them, and as weak as those who break them.

Jayd

Fantasy and illusion, reality and reason. Waves and particles. Energy and matter. Who is to say what is genius and what is insanity? What you believe is what is real for you. What matters is how your actions reflect your beliefs. What we know is only what we think we know.

As each day passed, the pieces of the puzzle began to interlock. There was a sense of purpose and meaning behind the presence of the alters, and compassion and healing as well. It was one of the hardest parts of the journey to understand because it didn't fit what Rebecca knew of herself. It wasn't rational or logical or under her control. It was much more.

Lynn brought stability and strength.

Water Girl brought back beauty and sensory experience.

Peter Pan was fun and playful.

Kat taught a powerful lesson about the meaning of freedom.

Each personality took her one step closer to the bridge, and showed her the first glimpses of the love coming from the other side; and that there was plenty of love on this side as well.

But she could not find her bridge bearing the heavy weight of labels. Was she creative, imaginative, crazy or confused? Could she separate herself from these alters surfacing from within? Would she want to? Questions without answers.

In truth, the nearer you are to the bridge, the less it matters.

Guides and Guidance

It's now Labor Day weekend and I've been off work since the middle of July. It feels like we spent the summer in a bubble, protected from the world and allowed our privacy. There has been no interference from anyone. No fallout from the family party. Not a word from my parents or from Thom. It is a mystery to me, but I'm grateful for this time to heal.

I still see Dr. Allen three times a week and we discuss events and personalities, but most of the work is done with my friends and the girls in the evening or the middle of the night, or at the cottage on weekends. Those are the times when the parts and pieces within me feel free to express – not in the short 50-minute sessions with a doctor who has only met a couple of them.

But I can forget all that on this three-day weekend, as the lake is alive with boaters and swimmers filling themselves with the last of the summer fun. We spend Saturday eating, sun-bathing and swimming. I rest at the picnic table as the sun sets and we prepare for the evening bonfire and roasted marshmallows. The girls pull lake toys onto the shore and change from wet swimsuits into long pants and shirts. Sean and Molly are in the cottage as I soak up the stillness and watch lights go on around the lake. I love this time of night when the energy shifts from humming boat motors and laughing, splashing kids to a mirrored finish on the lake and frogs harmonizing together in the background. How lucky I am to have this with my friends.

When Monday comes too soon, we grudgingly give up the long weekend. The next day I spend time quietly in my apartment until the girls get home from their first day of school and Molly and Sean get home from work.

Tonight we are all together again as the girls chat about classes and teachers and friends they haven't seen in months. Sean, Molly and I move to the basement to play pool and wait for another personality to arrive, and it isn't long before Peter Pan crawls around the legs of the pool table. Sean puts his pool cue away and reclines on the couch along the wall, while Molly tries to get Peter to talk to her. But Peter is feeling feisty tonight and wants to play. In his mind, Sean is a powerful dragon and the dragon must be conquered. Peter charges Sean, like a playful kitten, and then retreats to safety under the pool table.

"Come and fight me!" Peter challenges. "I can beat the mighty dragon! I will win!"

But there is no response from Sean. He's not interested in battle. Back and forth Peter dances, trying to get the dragon's response. Finally, Peter gives up and sulks in the corner. And so I sit on the cold tile floor with Peter. For a long time.

It's hard to keep up with all the activity and all the alters who come in as bits and pieces, but we've come to know some of them very well. Some are solid and full of life. Some are just wisps that appear with a message and fade away. But it's the guides that we rely on for information and understanding. I don't explain them. I just know we would be very confused without them.

The following Saturday, at the cottage, we get a visit from what appears to be a very powerful guide. I name her Celeste because she feels celestial to me and because her effect on Molly and Sean is visible. A palpable energy surrounds the three of us, and it is reflected in the expressions of my friends. She is obviously not an alter.

"This experience is a greater vision than you realize." Celeste says gently, "Yes, it is about healing the body and the mind, and even the spirit, but you are guided toward a new way of life that will go beyond what you can see now. You three are united, and connected to a Consciousness that flows through everyone's lives and calls to them in their minds and hearts. You witness now the disintegration of a false life and the opening of spiritual essence. You cannot change the course."

As she speaks, in my mind I see a powerful dam with water surging against it. The dam is strong, but water punishes it in angry bursts, hammering and unrelenting, pounding and dangerous.

"The dam will soon burst." Celeste says. Then she leaves me to explain my vision to my friends. And when she leaves we are in awe of the energy that was here and is now quite obviously gone.

The next few evenings, alters and guides are merciless. My world spins with personalities, divinity, and fantasy. It doesn't make sense in the world I knew, but as terrifying and confusing as it is, I would not go back. I can't go back. The guides say I can't push. I can't break the dam myself, but it will be broken when the time is right. Be patient. Trust. Let the alters express or progress will end.

I want to make space for the alters, yet I fight them. I do, but I don't. There's no room in my old life for any of this, but I can't flip the switch and make it stop. It's time to decide, and maybe commit to it.

Later in the week, as Molly, Sean and I relax in their living room, we're taken by surprise by a new alter. One even more unusual than most. My impression is that he's no more than 6 inches tall, very round and very animated. He enters my mind quickly and decisively and peers at the foreign world that surrounds him. He's tiny and curious and extremely quick. And has wings! He thinks he's inside a tree and that colors are dull here and movement is slow. Soon, however, he discovers my friends and starts talking.

"Well, hello! I'm Flit! Peter's friend Flit. I come here from our world."

"What does your world look like?" Molly is indulgent.

"Oh, there are beautiful flowers and trees and it's very green and open. But you have to watch out! There is danger, especially at night. But Peter keeps us safe. Peter is the boy who never sleeps. At night, we fairies roost in the trees, among the leaves where we blend in perfectly. Only Peter knows we are there."

Then Flit chuckles, "That boy! Very early in the morning, when I'm asleep, Peter sometimes sneaks up and slowly pulls down on the branch where I've made my bed. Then he lets it go and flings me into the air!"

Sean and Molly smile as Flit chats, barely taking a breath. Then suddenly he's gone, I'm thrown back into my own senses, and the room returns to normal. I have no explanation, just a new level of appreciation for my friends' indulgence. Dr. Allen says that without Molly and Sean, progress would be slow. I believe that without them, there would be no progress. There would be no one to play with Peter, or listen to the Little Ones, or let my internal world exist. There would be no safe place for personalities and no healing. There would certainly be no magic and no evolution of a world that I never knew existed in my mind. Crazy as it seems, these parts have become real to us all.

Lynn comes in later and says Flit is in trouble for sneaking out and talking too much, so he's home now nursing his wounded feelings. I have no idea who he answers to. And I don't know who is scary enough in Flit's world to keep Peter always on alert and never able to sleep. But, for now at least, there are no answers to my many questions.

Waking Up

"Every person is born with treasures," Lynn says, "Self-respect, self-worth, strength, generosity, compassion, kindness. It is a parent's job to show their children their treasures. 'These are yours!' they should say, 'and they are beautiful!' It's a terrible parent who doesn't see treasures in their children. Rebecca's treasures should have been given to her when she was little. One day, she'll decide how to claim and use them. Right now, she comes to you for help with the pain, and that's good. Her old defenses won't work anymore."

She speaks, as always, to me through Sean and Molly. Tonight she reprimands me. "You make change and growth hard and painful! Because if it isn't painful, you won't change. It doesn't have to be hard. You can resist and slow it down if you want, by being stubborn, but I don't recommend it. It's time to change your tools for living, your way of thinking. You'll find your treasures when it's time. Hold onto them. When the dam breaks, try to move to the side. Don't take the flood head on. And listen to Celeste! She'll be back. Pay attention!"

And then a surprise. "I'm leaving now. I don't know if I'll come back. Maybe," she says with a little smile, "just maybe I'm one of your treasures."

I don't want to believe she's gone. She's been such a huge part of our journey.

Celeste does return later this evening, as Lynn promised. "The dam is cracked and weakening. Hold onto at least one of your treasures when it breaks. What is outside will not help. It must be found within. No questions. No resistance. You have the key to the treasures, but understand that your friends are comfort, not safety. I will return to you. I will not let you face this alone."

I'm left with my thoughts and some emptiness at Lynn's swift good-bye. The guides say I need to learn to trust and to ask for help. And, even though I say that past actions were a long time ago and just insignificant moments, I justified too many insignificant moments. My life is made of these moments.

The guides tell us that I learned early that anger meant I was bad and deserved punishment, so I was responsible for that anger and punishment. How crushing for a child to feel responsible for an adult's anger. I know that the feelings, and burdens, in the little ones within me are my own. They cut through the years and the justification. Their feelings are pure and real and heartbreaking, and when they're here they melt my defenses. Their feelings are true and uncensored and I can't deny them.

When Dad used the willow switch on me, it reinforced his feelings about me. He didn't spend time with me, didn't hug me, didn't talk to me, didn't care who I was, didn't tell me he loved me. The only time I had his full attention was when he was angry, and that was brutal. I must write to him tonight. I must be honest and set my feelings free.

> *You gave me a legacy of pain with that willow switch.*
> *You stripped my trust, my security and my self-worth.*
> *You touched me in anger, not love. My body was little*
> *and my soul was delicate. You injured both. After that*
> *day, anger and pain were the same and all touch hurt.*
> *After that day, happy and sad were the same. There was*
> *no more freedom. It wasn't safe to make mistakes. You*
> *gave me guilt. I was guilty not only of disappointing you,*
> *but of being a bad person. I have struggled since that*
> *day to prove myself worthy of love. But I have always*
> *fallen short because you never let me know that I was,*
> *am, lovable – and that there is forgiveness.*
>
> *You passed your own pain to me. With one event*
> *you stole my childhood and you shaped my destiny. And*
> *with your lifelong reinforcement, you proved your intent.*

You left me that day blaming myself and feeling responsible for your anger. And you never told me otherwise. You let me continue to turn your anger in upon myself. I learned to be responsible for everyone's feelings but I could not trust my own.

You hurt me in so many ways, but I could never express that because you taught me to keep my feelings hidden and under control. I hated myself for even having those feelings. And I was sure that no one else could love me either.

But the legacy stops here.

What survived: appreciation, dignity, integrity, sensitivity, consideration, desire, determination, motivation... and hope...

Breaking the Shell

I went to my office today to take a birthday present to Angie. It's another world now after these past two months. I was only there a few minutes, but my boss called later and said I disrupted my co-workers and I was not to come into the department again until my return to work. They see nothing obviously wrong with me. They have no idea.

Celeste visits daily now. She says the dam represents my defenses and it's breaking. The Little One blocks the door to the treasures. She built a strong shell so she wouldn't be hurt. When the shell is broken, the dam will break. It would be best if she could break the shell herself. It will be by her choice, there will be less pain, and the lessons learned will be stronger.

"The shell was created from mistrust, frustration, and fear, and when it breaks, the power of the past will be gone."

On September 16, I attend a mandatory program at the Friend of the Court office. It feels like waking up in the middle of the divorce, churning feelings and memories again. Thom has kept his distance all these months. He doesn't challenge me on anything. Last spring, when I moved out, I expected, hoped maybe, that he would be more assertive. That he would compromise, change, fight for us. But he hasn't. He is no longer active in my life, except for the days he has the girls, and they handle that themselves. They don't share with me what happens during their time together. They protect me as I protect them.

The next day, Sean, Molly and I walk at a park a few miles from town with a wonderful hiking trail. Paths circle around a pond, over hills and across little bridges where streams trickle their way to the river. Today, as we walk, we meet an alter named Abby. She is very insecure and vigilant.

"I am part of her, but not from a specific time or place. I am made of emotions... fear, caution, apprehension, and others.

Those feelings are like a protective shell and they kept her safe, but they no longer serve her. Use trust, love, comfort and security to break the shell. Trying to break it from the outside, with reason and logic, will only strengthen it. The Little One has been listening and learning. Rebecca now understands what created the shell and it has been broken and the dam is crumbling. I... am...free."

Abby is gone, but the Little One comes in to explain. "I lived inside for a long time. Abby, the shell, watched over me and protected me. But I'm not afraid anymore."

As she speaks, she grows more mature and confident. Her voice and tone change. Then, she melts into me and I feel somehow fuller, richer.

Sean understands. "The Little One has self-confidence now and has broken the shell, and when she got it, you got it too."

So, the shell was an alter and has merged with me. I assume the dam is coming down soon, just as Celeste warned us.

In the meantime, other guides come to help us. They say I must listen to them and they will teach me. I must believe there are no obstacles, only opportunities. "There are many paths to take, but, ultimately, peace is found within. Do not question or deny what is within you. Listen to your heart and learn to use these alters and guides as tools. Close the past and stop looking back."

They say the dam was reinforced by sandbags of insecurity, subordination, expectations, responsibility, and self-imposed burdens. When I recognize and understand these burdens, they will be removed. I strengthen my treasures by believing in them, just as I strengthen the dam with old beliefs.

I try to understand all this. I try to accept it, but it's another layer to decipher. Sean and Molly and I simply listen now. It is what it is.

A week later, Bunny comes in during a long walk with Sean and Molly at the park. She says she took fear for me until I was able to handle it myself. As we walk, she changes and her voice loses the little girl tremor. Sean and Molly stop and we wait for Bunny to finish. She says she stopped "growing" recently when I began to confront my fears. And she says I should not feel guilty. Guilt knows just how to hurt, and feasts on worry and shame. She says it's very hard for an alter to come through when guilt is present. Then she mists into me.

Bunny is yet another personality who goes away as I wait for the dam to break, whatever that may mean. The guides say I can slow things down, and maybe I am. Change is hard and there has been so much of it. But I need stability because Dr. Allen is returning me to work in two weeks. He's not comfortable keeping me on sick leave any longer, he says, and I guess I agree with him. I am healthier since our friends have nurtured me so well. But how can I spend eight hours a day in a cubicle with alters and guides? How can I merge these worlds?

Just A Little Mutiny

I feel as dreary as the weather in these last days of September. I hate for winter to come, and it already feels cold and lonely and gray. Alters and guides are constantly in my mind, my life. And I still occasionally waiver between missing Thom and trying to be excited about being on my own once the divorce is final.

My mood affects the girls, too, because tonight they are argumentative and disgusted with the past months of disruption, and they take turns discharging their unhappiness and their frustration. They don't want to live with Sean and Molly anymore. They want a normal life, girl time, and the freedom I promised them when we left Thom. They want to count on me and talk to me without triggering another personality. They're afraid to share with me because I've been so fragile. And they feel left out. They want to tell me about their day and their feelings and their problems.

I'm not surprised that they're finally confronting me. They want me back, and their needs got lost. There is no routine, no answers, and no security for them. We're constantly with Sean and Molly and Ann, and I don't blame Lee and Elizabeth for being sick of it. Promises of a normal life are all pretense now and they know it. There are no guarantees and no sign of ending. When the alters or guides come in, the girls automatically leave us to handle it. They know Sean and Molly will take care of whatever might happen, but it doesn't matter. They're still left out and I always come first.

"And why does Ann get to know everything and we don't!" Lee asks. There are tears in Elizabeth's eyes, along with determination, but Lee shows only exasperation.

So now I know that against my wishes, Sean and Molly tell Ann about our conversations with the guides and alters. Ann, of course, then tells Elizabeth and Lee. I would do the same if the

135

situation was reversed, but it makes it harder to avoid pulling the girls into my problems. It also gives Ann an edge when she already has more control. After all, it's her house and her cottage, and we depend on her parents. So when Ann knows, it seems that I don't trust my girls like Sean and Molly trust Ann.

"I'm so sorry." It's the best I can give them tonight. "I'm sorry this is happening. Ann isn't supposed to know any of it either. I have no control over what Molly and Sean tell her, but I just don't want you to have to deal with it. I'm trying to protect you from all this! It's not fun for me either, and I'm afraid. I wish I could make it stop, but there's no stopping it now. It's gone too far. We can't go back. We have to move ahead and hope for the best."

I'm beginning to panic. I don't have the strength for this right now. Pressure is building and I'm losing ground. Is this when the dam breaks? Now? With the girls? How will they deal with that? I can't let it happen now, whatever it may be. Not with just the girls here. I still have to protect them.

"Get your coats, girls, and get into the car. We're going to Sean and Molly's for the night. I need to talk to them."

Lee storms out of the apartment with Elizabeth behind her. But they get it. They know I'm not well and I'm nervous about returning to work. They know the game. But they've spent way too much time with our friends. They've known them all their lives, but not as authorities and certainly not so consistently. We all simmer in silent frustration as I drive, and I pray that no alter comes in. When we get there, the girls grab Ann and head for the basement without a backward glance.

When I bring it up to them, Molly and Sean offer no apologies for telling Ann, and I ask for none. I have no right to tell them what to do. They've done so much to help me.

The Waiting Game

The next evening, I sit alone in the apartment while Lee and Elizabeth visit with Thom. The girls and I are fine now, after they had their chance to vent and have their feelings validated. They've been so patient with all these months of confusion. I'm glad they had their say, but still sorry that I must cling to our friends.

There is rare silence and solitude here tonight. Time to think and process, which doesn't happen often. My thoughts move to Lee and Elizabeth. The girls deserve better than they're getting from me. I need to find a way to settle down and to be in control again. I'll go back to work soon and this unpredictable craziness absolutely cannot happen there. I refuse to let it take over my life any longer. I just have to buckle down and get stronger. I can beat this!

Suddenly, I can't move. I try to turn my head, but I can't. I can't even move my eyes! Finally, with monumental effort, I grasp the phone that is right next to me. I force my fingers to curl around it and push the buttons with the knuckle of my other hand. What's going on! Sean answers the phone, but I cannot speak. Tears well up as I sit silently with the phone at my ear. And then...

"My business is with her." And my finger pushes the disconnect button.

When Molly and Sean walk in about 10 minutes later, I'm staring at the curtains. I can't talk or move and I've gone from fear to fuming, but it doesn't matter. So I sit and wait. And wait. And wait for what feels like forever. But, as always, Sean and Molly just go with it, and they wait, too. It's gone beyond frustrating for me because I am using all my mental energy to control my body, and nothing works. This is ridiculous! I feel like a scolded child sitting in "time out." Finally my head turns toward my patient friends.

"She is holding up progress. If she does not stop her busywork, she will be stuck in her old life. She has been focusing on trivial matters and not listening to what we tell her. Our work with her is important and she must take it seriously. She is not in charge anymore."

As they let me return, I am furious. Sean just relaxes and laughs at their creativity. Of course.

"Well," he says, "I think I'd pay attention from now on if I were you! Time to listen to them or next time you might not get off so easy."

They are quiet the rest of the week. It's an eerie internal silence and a calm that I have not felt since June, as though they've released me. It's strange, though. It doesn't seem right. I should be happy to have control of my mind and my thoughts and my actions, but now I feel abandoned. What have they done to me?

On Sunday night, after pizza with our friends, I finally feel the familiar sensation of a guide.

"She tucked her emotions away, as a child. Every time she felt any emotion that wasn't safe to express, she placed it into a 'mood bucket.' And so she was a 'moody' child. It covered everything. But now she must dump the mood bucket, separate the emotions, and name them. She was expected to be a China doll with no emotions, and so that's what she became." There is a pause, and then...

"What does it take to crush a child's spirit?"

The following Tuesday night is dark and rainy. We spend yet another evening at Sean and Molly's because I want to give my personalities as much time as possible to resolve their issues, and to communicate and do whatever else they need, before I go back to work in two days. So I'm happy when I feel the gentle but powerful energy of a guide.

"It is a vile and vicious thing to manipulate a child and to own them. That damage runs deep and remains hidden there. The child will learn blame, shame, guilt, worthlessness, and failure.

The child will learn to depend on others for her value. She was without choice. She could not say no, or ask why, or make mistakes and learn from them. There was no independence and no forgiveness. She had little confidence, few skills, and no strength to sustain her in life. And she had an abusive marriage because she had an abusive childhood. She does not know, still, her own needs or pleasures. She tried to please her parents, but felt she failed. It was their game, and they could change the rules. But it was no game to her."

When the guide is gone, I hear the echo of my father's words: *You should have known! What were you thinking? You're too sensitive. I'll tell you when to be happy and I'll tell you when to be sad.* He made it hard for me to believe in myself.

The guide's words are painful... and true. I couldn't win with my father, or with Thom. The rules changed and the expectations rose. I did sacrifice my needs and minimized my opinions and desires. And I let them rule. I see that now.

There has been no more talk about the dam, but I don't need anything else to think about right now. It hurts to see what I couldn't see before. How could I not have realized how I was set up in my childhood to believe that emotional abuse was tolerable? "You can't see it and still live in it," the guides have said. And now they have dropped the first domino that knocks down all the rest. The past changes with any new information. Memories come apart. The whole tapestry unravels.

Liza

The mind of a child is fragile. Every moment a new beginning. The sun is brighter, green is greener, love is fresh and words are literal. Removing the magic from a child's mind in the name of education is a weak and selfish act. It is the act of someone who wants to shape that child into their image, their beliefs, and make that child easier to control. It is a lazy, intentional and systematic manipulation of the truth of that child's perfection. You were born beautiful and continue to be beautiful in the heart of creation. You were born to love and be loved, not to perpetuate a sad dream of imperfection and hate. You know within you that this is true. It is the influence of others that causes you to doubt it.

Jayd

The teaching is obvious now. Everything was shining a light on the past and gleaning the treasures that were left there. Every step was one more away from old lessons and into a future of freedom. Rebecca could not see the big picture at the time, of course. That would have stripped the magic from the incredible journey she was taking. As they say, most adventures are only fun after they're over.

It's still a miracle to me how the whole trip was so divinely choreographed. Everything brought enlightenment... especially the dismantling of old truths. Each personality and guide allowed her to expand beyond what she knew, even as she struggled with it.

Every moment was filled with love and compassion, even as it was disguised as pain.

Water Over The Dam

I'm back to work, not by choice, but by necessity. I still tell myself I need control of my life again to give the girls some normalcy. My mind thinks returning to work is the right thing to do. My heart isn't convinced. But this is a new day and I'm determined to handle it. Co-workers oddly act as though I never left, and alters do not push today. But I still feel like I'm standing on the edge of a cliff.

The girls and I are, of course, back with our friends tonight. I'm anxious for any insights the guides or alters may have about my day, but, as usual, when a guide does arrive, it's all about the interminable breaking of the dam.

"One more event and there will be revelation. The dam stands only from habit and leans in on itself. She must hold onto the treasures. The break will happen quickly. It is the ending and the beginning. She must be prepared."

This information doesn't help today. I feel trapped, once again, between two worlds. There is the world of bills, responsibility, and caretaking. And then the other one. Guides and personalities and alters and fairies and children and on and on and on it goes. I don't know fantasy from reality anymore.

On Friday night, I'm grateful to have made it through two days at work without incident. Molly, Sean and I sit on the burnt orange-colored carpeting near the open stairway to their bedroom. The personality trying to enter is probably one of the little ones because they often seek a safe place on the floor.

This one comes forward as an angel-child, and in my mind I see her, perfect and protected, in a white house. She is special, sweet and pure. No wonder I kept this little part safely tucked away.

"I am Ruby Red," she says shyly. She feels like soothing balm.

Sean eases in closer and Ruby Red raises wide eyes to take in this large man who is now slightly threatening. She's afraid of him. He knows it, too, and doesn't want to frighten her. He gives her a few minutes and then, very gently and slowly, his hand slides across the carpet toward her. Immediately he has her full attention. He's moving and she is ready to shift back inside, but I don't want her to go. She feels like heaven. Sean raises his index finger and waggles it a little. Then his middle finger wiggles a bit and then the two fingers begin a little dance, and Ruby Red is transfixed. When the dance ends, she looks up at him and smiles. And then she fades away and I am plunked back into reality. I am a lead weight without her, and out of tune. If Ruby Red is part of me, it's a part I'm willing to fight for.

Immediately, a guide surfaces to warn us. They don't want her hurt - and she could be easily wounded. I know immediately what they mean, and that the slightest spill of the toxic waste of my emotional state would destroy her. She is not an age or a personality or an emotion - she is an undamaged state of being, guileless and unspoiled.

The next morning, Sean fixes Sunday breakfast for me and Molly while the girls still sleep in Ann's room. After breakfast, Sean goes to shower and Molly settles into a chair with a book. I sit in the sunlight of the southern window, thinking about work tomorrow and hoping the week will be uneventful.

And then it comes upon me like lava. It starts in my stomach, a ball of burning energy, and climbs into my throat. Memories, regrets, guilt, anger, resentment, disgust, all ride the crest of this massive, crushing force. I am dragged inside where I see a gargantuan mountain of a dam bombarded by the hostile hammering of water. Over and over, powerful waves smash into the decaying mammoth until the dam gives way in an explosion of devastation. Years of repressed emotion released at once.

I built that dam, layer by layer, crafted under the instruction of my father. He was the architect, but I built it by my own hand with beliefs I was taught. Years of esteem-shattering assumptions. One by one, the emotions went behind the dam until I believed I had none. That I could survive on books and solitude and the idea that people were either to be obeyed or avoided. Memories pour over me, borne by the emotional flood of imprisoned truth. I choke with it and tumble round and round beneath the current.

"Find a treasure!" I hear from far away. "They said any one will save you!"

It's Sean. He and Molly are with me in the entryway of their house. I'm not sure how I got here, but my face is soaked with tears and I'm curled up and trembling in the corner by the door. Treasure?

"I can't think of anything!" I sob. There is no treasure in the bitter water in my mind.

"Tell us one good thing about yourself!" Molly pleads.

I can't think as I spin and flail in waves of pain.

"Tell us something good!" Molly demands, and I instinctively obey.

"I am, um, I am kind?…" I sniff, but it eases the raging force in my head. "I try to be nice…"

The current slows and I scramble within my mind toward shore where a huge Victorian house sits majestically on the bank of the churning river. A white house so big and stable that no force could ever move it, and the river cannot reach it. But as I climb from the river, the picture fades. The energy eases and I focus on my friends' faces. I wipe tears from my chin and attempt to explain what just happened.

"It was real! As real as you and I are real right here! Water and the white house! I made it!" But, it doesn't matter. They can't understand. It is not their journey and not their reality. Molly hands me some tissues and as I pick myself up I understand that nothing has changed for them, but everything has changed for me.

143

I'm in a hard place, thinking about it all the next morning as I drive to work. The dam is gone. I felt it break. But I get the metaphor. Moving on is not easy, though. Today the colors of the leaves on the trees in the parking lot at work are bright gold and orange against the blue October sky. The seasons move on. Loose leaves twitter in the steady breeze and run across the pavement as they escape their branches. They are between green and gone. And I am between worlds, too. It's time to commit to my new life. How can I reconcile these two worlds, though? The old and the new are mixed. I am not whole yet.

Molly stopped by our apartment last night and said she's tired of shoveling shit. She didn't want Sean to know she was there and we talked at the door away from the girls. She is not pulling away from me, she said, but she has to take care of her family, too. It was hard for her to say, but it was a warning as well. She's concerned that Sean's getting too close to me, too involved in my problems. Of course, she is. I would feel the same and I doubt I could have done as much as they have done. I'm sure she's happy I'm back to work. I've disrupted their lives for months, kept them awake at night, put them through the monotonous tumult of my childhood and generally been a constant challenge. I'm sure they're over the novelty and well on their way toward saturated.

I sit in my cubicle, thinking about the changes in my life this year. I have to tell management, and my co-workers, why I've been off work for three months. I can't let an alter come in and take them by surprise. But how do I explain dissociative identity disorder and still keep my credibility? I have to trust that they'll support me and at least try to understand. No alters have come in here, but I have no guarantee they won't.

I take a deep breath and glance at Alma and Marcia chatting together quietly. This will take all my courage. I move to the aisle next to the empty cubicles of Angie and Bella, who have probably gone to lunch. Maybe it'll be easier if I only tell two at a time. This will spread quickly through the company, but it has to be done.

"Um, hi..."

Alma stops talking and Marcia stands up with a smile, so I plunge ahead.

"I've got to tell you something." How do I make this not threatening? "I want you to know why I've been off work for so long. And so you won't be surprised later on. It's pretty interesting, actually, and I'm dealing with it, but I think it's something you should know about."

Don't choke... don't stop...

"You know that I'm going through a divorce and it's been pretty hard on me. I've never been through anything like this and it hit me harder than I expected. And then some other things started happening and my life's been pretty crazy since June. I went to the doctor and he says I have dissociative identity disorder. It used to be called multiple personality disorder. I think it's because of all the stress. I'm sure it will work itself out with some time. I'm sure it will all be just fine and..."

Suspicious stares and then walls snap up, and our conversation is over. *Very smooth, Rebecca.* No explanation will suffice now and I retreat to my desk. I didn't know what to expect and I understand, I suppose, but I'm also disappointed and even more nervous. Compassion would have been nice. Well, it's too late to go back now. I can only hope for the best.

As I meet with managers and other co-workers the rest of the day, sharing as few specific details as possible, I'm greeted with varying degrees of curiosity, skepticism, and, finally, distance. No one wants to be associated with this. My manager says the company will work with me, but they have to be careful about disrupting the department. As long as I do my work and show up on time, there isn't much they can do. After all, I haven't done anything wrong. But I leave my boss's office feeling diminished and fragile.

Then I see that Angie, my unshakable friend, is waiting for me. She hustles me to the cafeteria, away from the choking corporate rigidity and private judgments, and asks for more information. She wants to know what's really going on. I explain what I can, what the last three months have meant and how I've changed, and I watch her eyes for an honest reaction. I see that she truly is curious, unafraid and open-minded. *Thank you, Angie, for your strength.* Sometimes it only takes one person who believes in you to give you the courage to believe in yourself again.

I haven't felt strong these past months. I've been surviving and always on the edge of panic. But survival takes strength, too. It will take much more courage in the future for me to step into the light than to remain cowering in the darkness. I must choose the light.

Liza

As children, you are taught not to see what your eyes show you and not to hear what reaches your ears. You are taught to behave in ways that are counter to your truth. Your heart expands when you look, hear, and speak honestly. It contracts when you are taught to ignore or devalue your own senses. Soon, though, you no longer listen to the heart, as it will not argue with your world. And then your being gets caught in small thoughts, manipulations, and beliefs, and you are trapped in confusion. It is no wonder that you waiver between faith and fear. Yet, the only thing to fear in the world is how you perceive it. Nothing is solid or dangerous or final. Peace rests in how much you are willing to release your perceptions and in how little you decide to honor the game.

Jayd

We all play the social games. We change depending on who we're with. You know it's true when your worlds collide. When friends meet family, and co-workers meet partners, and professional relationships become personal. How hard it often is to maintain so many different lives. How often do we compromise ourselves for others? And, if we change depending on who we're with, then who are we really? Are we composites of their expectations? Do we become who they expect to see?

Rebecca could no longer pretend. Not for others, but especially not for herself. The images were fading, along with the strength to maintain them. There is no honor in minimizing yourself just to get along. It takes courage and strength to live from your heart.

There comes a point when you can no longer live with the lies and still be at peace with yourself.

Amelia Of The Path

As mid-October turns more leaves to red and orange, I'm more cautious now with Molly and Sean. Molly and I have an understanding, and our friendship is solid, but I am more vigilant of the space I take up in their lives.

After work today, we walk in the park on the familiar path along the river. It's a gorgeous fall day, and I love strolling beneath the giant trees and over the little bridges. But I am not myself now. I have shifted and, even though my own hair is short and dark, I feel long sandy brown strands licking my cheeks and tickling my neck. I have become tiny, supple and willowy. A soft breeze I hadn't noticed a minute ago perks up my nostrils and I smell river and moss and the rotting roots of wonderfully aged trees. I'm in heaven on this well-worn dirt path, which has suddenly come to life. I dance ahead of Sean and Molly, twirling and high from the scent of the woods.

"Ruby Red can't go out, but I do what I want."

"Do you know Ruby Red?" Sean asks, ready for the next character, as always.

"Of course," she says, as my mind is flooded with images of a place I've seen twice. It is the white Victorian house, but this time an unkempt child crouches beneath a window. She is the girl I have now become, tattered and tanned, alert and on guard. She speaks furtively with Ruby Red, who sits calmly, beautiful and perfect, on the other side of the window. They are mirror images in size and facial features, but worlds apart in awareness and expression. I can't hear their conversation, but they see me. They are discovered.

As the path takes a sudden turn toward the river, my mind returns to the moment and the onslaught of sensation.

"I love the river." She's not shy at all, like Ruby Red is. "And I *love* paths because they both go places."

"Do you live by the river?" Molly asks.

"I live outside of the big white house. I never go inside. Ruby Red can't talk to the outdoors. Ruby Red can't do anything – she is kept inside."

As we walk, I continue to embrace amazing sensations while I listen to her joyful chatter. These woods hum and breathe, and the river sings and I'm aware of the life that could not exist anywhere else. We're in a fantasy that no picture could describe. How could you paint the life force, the magic, the wonder of this place? How could I not have seen it before, or realized what it gives to us with each visit?

"Do you have a name?" Sean asks. She doesn't answer, preferring nature over people.

"How about 'Amelia'?" he coaxes. She is pleased with the way the sound of this name rolls like the wild hills. Amelia.

Solidly rooted now, Amelia decides to share.

"They took her," she says. "And she couldn't see the trees and flowers." Amelia skips up the pathway and calls back. "But she is starting to listen to the world again."

She flashes a huge smile, enthralled with her own communication. Did we know that trees whisper at night so they don't wake the birds? That the birds wake up the trees in the morning? And, by the way, did we know that she lives in a hole in the bottom of a big tree?

Suddenly we're off the path and blazing a new trail sharply to the left and away from the river. Amelia has forgotten Sean and Molly. She wants to explore and meet the trees further off the path. The ones that no one really sees. Sean and Molly lag behind as Amelia runs. Around and through and behind and over and under we go. My body is not my own and Amelia has much more stamina than I do. More proof to me that the state of my body is dependent on the state of my mind. I'm very much as old as I feel, yet Amelia is in great shape.

She scampers up onto the huge trunk of a fallen tree, drops down straddling it and gazes back toward the river. She would stay in these woods forever if she could, but, finally, it's time to leave. The day is cooling and we have to go home.

"You have to let her come back now." Sean says, "It's time for us to leave."

"Yap, yap, yap," says Amelia distractedly. Molly chuckles, but Sean keeps trying.

"Amelia, it's time to go. Would you like a ride in our big, blue truck?"

"Yap, yap, yap."

I'm tired of this little pixie and ready for her to leave, and I'm sure Molly and Sean are hungry.

"The park is closing soon," Sean tells her, "and they will make us go home."

Amelia drags each foot behind her as she reluctantly follows him to the truck. She looks at the truck curiously. Apparently she, who has never entered this world, has never seen a vehicle. I feel her wavering on the decision to leave the park, as Sean continues to try to entice her to climb through the open door. It takes some firmness, and even a bit of scolding, before she actually steps up and slides into the center of the bench seat.

At last we're headed home, but Amelia is so imbedded that she shows no signs of leaving, even when the speed of the truck makes her stomach turn. Oh, god, Amelia's carsick. Why won't she just leave!! I feel her queasiness, but I also feel sorry for poor Amelia, small and forlorn, caught and taken from her beloved outdoors.

"I want to get out." Amelia whines to herself as she wistfully watches the trees speed by.

We make it to my friends' house without making a mess in their truck, and find the girls watching TV. Even though I know they want time with me to share their day, Amelia is still in charge. We file past them and into the basement where Sean and Molly try to decipher Amelia's purpose. Amelia is very unhappy as she looks at the fine wooden paneling on the walls. She blurts accusingly, "These trees are dead!"

I see the four walls through her eyes and feel trapped. I wish Amelia would go back home, or find comfort here, but she is a wildflower and will not bloom indoors. She wheedles and whines and pleads with Sean and Molly to let her go. They can't, they say, because Rebecca would not want to leave.

We know from experience that Amelia has a purpose. We just need to find it. An hour later, Amelia recedes and we gratefully go upstairs where I claim the girls and go home.

The next day, I struggle to stay myself at work. I feel internal pushes occasionally and I plead with my personalities to wait until it's safe. Co-workers are careful around me. They're not sure what to say or do, and I can just imagine the conversation when I'm not around. It would only take one event to trigger an office landslide.

This afternoon I have a training class and I have my brain firmly locked in. I must focus. I will be strong. And I feel normal for the first hour of class. Then, just as class ends, the light in the room waivers and I feel myself thinning. I grab the edge of the table and stare at the keyboard. *Oh, no, you don't!! Push, damn it!!! Push them out! Keep them out!!! I WILL hold on!*

I run out the door as soon as we're dismissed, while I still have some control, but a co-worker leaves with me. Just great! I really need an audience right now. I stop in the hallway and she stops, too. I know she's heard about me. Everyone knows, just like I knew they would. But her expression breaks my awareness of the burning energy flow for a second. I see kindness, and sympathy. The thought that she can be trusted zips by, and then words come pouring out of me. It's an unknown alter and there is no one here to name her.

"I hate all this restriction! I hate to be told what to do, when to do it and how! It's just like when she was a kid!"

As the words tumble out, old sensations wash over me, like a parade from the past: suffocation, dependency, despair, hope, fear, anger, desire and hopelessness.

"She could never please him, never be enough. It was always about her father and his control."

More and more and more of my life spills out. My co-worker is the audience so that I can hear the words. I know how it works, but I am humiliated and can do nothing to stop it.

"Why are you here now?" The co-worker asks. "Why come here when she's at work?"

I stop the constant pacing that most of my alters need in order to stay in and look her in the eye.

"Ask her to compare what I just said with how she feels when she's at work. Ask her if she's putting her needs aside so she doesn't upset anyone. Ask her if she is being shut out in her department just like he shut her out when she didn't meet his expectations. If she's struggling to fulfill a role, to create an image. Ask her what she's afraid of if the alters come in."

And then there is more.

"What she is going through is an opportunity for those she works with to learn and grow, to open their minds and see beneath the surface, but most of them aren't taking advantage of it and, in fact, are determined not to."

And then the alter is gone and I am back.

"Ugh! I'm so sorry you had to hear all of that. It wasn't meant for you." I'm ready to leave. Quit. Hide.

"You have to do what you have to do. You can't worry about what people say," she says, and leaves me with a hug. That's easy to say when you don't have to face it. Why do I have to deal with people anyway? Why can't I just work through this my way?! I have to get out of here. I need to think and I can't do it here. I feel like a fish in a bowl.

The closer I get to my desk, the more the anger and the frustration flow and get bigger and bigger until I'm red hot and consumed by it. It's everywhere and I'm everywhere and I'm afraid because the power of it is overwhelming. Bella, one of the few who has accepted me as I am now, sees me come around the corner and hands me a message.

"Your daughter called…," but her voice trails off as I spin toward her. It isn't me anymore. I am rage and defiance and power and I turn it on her in a searing glare just as Marcia's head moves from where she was hidden from view behind Bella. Marcia peers around Bella with huge eyes. This is the behavior she's been waiting for. I grab my things and head for home, grateful for the weekend.

We spend Friday evening with Sean and Molly. Stress has increased tremendously with my return to work and the constant worry about what will happen there. And my fears are absolutely justified after today. But I live two lives now, and I've been through too much to let the people at work have this much control over my emotions. I would defy any of them to handle it any better. But my nerves are fried and my appetite is gone again.

After dinner, and feeling in control of myself for a minute, I gather the girls to leave. I'm looking forward to the rest of the evening with them and having the weekend to rest. Monday will bring more than I want to imagine right now.

We jump into the car and I can tell the girls are as excited about our weekend as I am. Elizabeth won "shotgun" tonight so she's in the front seat. It won't be long and we'll be cozied up with a movie and a snack.

I don't think we're a hundred yards down the road when I am no longer myself, time slows, and my foot eases off the accelerator. I know this feeling well, but which one is it?

"I want to go to the woods!" Oh, no! Amelia!! The girls have not met Amelia but I've told them about her.

Amelia is unconcerned that she is driving my car, but she isn't sure what to do. She sends a quick glance toward Elizabeth, and then her focus is on the line of trees growing about a quarter of a mile off the road to our left. If she turns the wheel in that direction, we'll be going into a ditch, through at least one fence and across an open expanse of planted field.

Elizabeth calls to me. "Mom, come back! Right now!" I hear Lee unbuckle and lean on the back of the seat behind me. "Mom, come back right now!!"

I swear to you, baby, I am trying!

"Amelia?" Lee inquires gently. "Is it you? Can you drive?" But Amelia is focused on the woods.

"Mom? Mom? *Mom!*" Elizabeth calls, but Amelia has no connection to them at all.

Then Elizabeth's voice rises an octave. *"Mom! Mom! Mom!!"*

We're only going about 10 miles an hour now, but Amelia wants to be free. Mmmm, trees! Wonderful, safe, friendly trees! Amelia expectantly observes the steering wheel as though, all by itself, it will do her bidding.

"Amelia, you can't go to the woods!" Lee commands. "Amelia, I want to drive now. Stop the car! Push on the brake pedal!"

"Mom! Mom! Come back!" I hear Elizabeth's voice climb to near hysteria, and I am using all my power to break Amelia's hold. I think we're wearing her down! And, finally, with a last longing look at the little forest, Amelia gives in and I come back, but I have had enough. It's been a long week and I don't want to play anymore. I have no idea, as usual, what will happen next, but with Amelia so close and so powerful, I will need Sean and Molly's help. Back we go to their house, and this time the girls are okay with that.

Worlds Collide

God DAMN it!! If you don't want to be here, then don't come in!!

But my thoughts have no power and Amelia catches Angie's eye as she eases out of my cubicle and around the corner. But what she seeks is not here. There are no birds drifting on the breeze, no scent of summer, no trees to cradle her with their strength. There is only dull gray and a maze of strange alleyways that lead nowhere. Amelia wants out and I can't influence her. I am not safe here, I realize. For the first time, it becomes very obvious how Sean and Molly protect me from myself, and from a potentially dangerous world. And, even more, I fully realize how vulnerable I am to the decisions of my alters. I've never felt so small and helpless.

Amelia spots a window and blue sky. As she moves toward it, Angie is behind her with a running stream of questions. Amelia looks at Angie, irritated with her presence, yet pleased that Angie is so interested in her.

"Who are you?" Angie asks. "What do you want? Where are you going?"

"I don't like it here," Amelia says, "I'm leaving."

"Oh, no!" Angie pleads. "No, you can't leave here. You have to stay. You have to let Rebecca come back and do her work. She needs to be here now. You can't go out of the building!"

"Yap, yap, yap," says Amelia.

We creep past empty cubicles whose occupants have thankfully gone to lunch. Angie follows, frantically trying to negotiate, when Amelia spots a toy. On the corner of the desk in an empty cubicle, shining temptingly, is a magnetic sculpture. There are a hundred star-shaped bits of metal attached to each other by a magnet in the base. Amelia pokes at it with one finger and then pulls the sculpture to her chest and dives under the desk.

Angie takes this opportunity to find reinforcements and soon she and an office coordinator named Jan watch me contentedly playing.

"You have to come with us," Jan says boldly, but her voice quivers and she's clearly not okay with this.

Amelia works her way from under the desk, believing someone has come to show her the way out.

"I want to go outside. I don't like it here."

She follows Jan into the manager's office, which only makes things worse because now we're next to a window. Amelia gazes longingly at the warm fall day and down the three stories to the street below. She's getting upset. I don't know why she's hanging on and pray that she'll tire and recede back into her own world.

Amelia rests her hands on the window and wonders why so many ugly buildings spoil the view. She feels claustrophobic, and desperation begins to surface and my feelings ride the wave with her. When people hear about this, no one will feel safe with me. There is no way that management will take a chance on the unpredictability. Amelia turns and finds her way blocked by Angie and Jan. She is almost in tears and our senses mingle in defeat. *You've ruined me, Amelia. We're going down together.*

In a last defiant strike, Amelia declares to Jan and Angie that they all buzz like their stupid place and she fades away. I come back in as Jan breaks down and her face melts into a stream of tears.

"It's just so sad," she says. "This all just makes me sad."

And then our boss Dana comes into the office.

"I have to go home," I tell her.

"Are you okay to drive?"

I lie and tell her I'm fine, but I have no freaking idea if I'm okay. I'm pretty sure I'm not okay, but I certainly can't stay here right now. I need out of here. She readily gives me the time off and in moments I'm safely in my car.

The Guides Guide

I shouldn't have worried about returning to work the next day after Amelia's appearance. No one wants to touch this and no one says a word, yet I walk on a razor's edge, feeling the pressure, waiting and wondering what will happen next. I call my friends in the afternoon and ask them to meet me at the park after work. Walking there is the best therapy I could have. Breathing in the breeze, listening to the birds, and the freedom of simply being outside is so much better than the fifty-minute scheduled sessions in the doctor's office.

It isn't long after we meet and take to the path that a guide comes in. I expect it. We rarely get out of here without someone coming in. It's another comfort spot where they can speak in peace.

"So many things are going on inside. She doesn't see that she struggles with an image created when she was little. She must see that it is not her truth, and the more she fights, the stronger it becomes. Let go and it will no longer exist."

These ideas, these suggestions of the guides, are as transparent as they are. Where are they in the real world? How can they help me at work, at home, in my life? Where are they when the mud flies and the bleeding starts! It pisses me off sometimes. How can these guides *really* help! Mostly they give me only vague, wispy messages and delicate strands of assurance.

But Molly cuts off my internal complaining and takes this opportunity to ask for more information.

"Who are the guides? How can we call on them for help?" But the guide just continues.

"She must *use* the energy. She should learn only a little at a time and have patience. The Others are helping and she will need their help until she can do it herself. She must learn to trust. You are her foundation until she builds her own. It took tremendous events to separate her into these many parts. It will take tremendous events to re-teach her. The guides are sorry for what will happen. If they could take the pain they would. But these events will become great gifts."

"How will she know what to do?" Molly asks.

"Trust her intuition. One day she will teach others how to feel and use their own intuition, and listen to their own internal guidance. They will be drawn to her for the teaching."

Trust my intuition. I don't trust anything about me these days. I have no control over any of it and apparently no choice in how I'm being used.

The rest of the walk is quiet and we finally return to our separate cars in the parking lot. I don't need to continue this aggravation at my friends' house. I need my kids and some hugs and maybe a little something to eat. Time to go home.

The next day is another quiet day on the job. Apparently the alters know there is no one at work who can or will listen to them the way Sean and Molly do, and I'm grateful they wait for tonight's peaceful evening with my friends. I am not angry now. It does no good to fight, since I seem to be always fighting myself. I'll be a good pupil again and... a guide slides in. I sit on the floor at the end of the couch where Sean reclines and Molly rests next to me, waiting as usual with a pen and pink paper. This time, though, the message is partially verbal and partially a vision.

"The shell broke into fragments," the guide tells my friends, "sharp fragments all around her. She inspects them when she finds them."

A picture forms in my mind: I am alone on a bare floor in a darkened room, sad and afraid. Scattered near me are various sizes of glass with beveled edges. The pieces of glass contain memories and pain. There are many colors and shapes, and light radiates from within them.

"She must be careful not to cut herself on these fragments by using the old tools. They, like the dam, have their purpose and fit together like a puzzle. The pieces are valuable – made of many different things. But they are very sharp. They are not dead - they can cut and hurt – and they bleed into her as she bleeds from them. She cannot neglect them, though, or their lives will end. They must find their proper place."

I get the message. Amelia's appearance at work, and yesterday's conversations in the park, make more sense now that I've calmed down and had time to think. The guide is saying that I need to use the past for strength and knowledge, not to hurt myself and others with old memories, resentment and guilt. And that each piece is an alter, alive and connected to me. If I learn from them, the puzzle will all fit together. If not, I will simply continue to cause myself pain.

The next day is a beautiful end to October, with colored leaves still clinging to the trees in vivid contrast to the blue sky. Soon, though, a big wind, a fall storm, will blow them into winter and the trees will sleep until spring. But today is an unusually warm Saturday and we need fresh air. There is no better place for that than the park, so Sean and Molly and I jump into the big blue truck early in the morning before the girls are out of bed. Even though we invite them along for the five-mile hike, they always seem to have something better to do.

Amelia accepts the invitation and pops in before we've barely stepped out of the truck, and off we go. She knows the paths now, between the trees, around the pond, and over the familiar bridges. On one bend of the path, near the edge of the river, Amelia spots a tiny trail made by raccoons or skunks or some other nocturnal creature of the woods and, on hands and knees, we follow it. *Gross!! It stinks down here!* Amelia giggles to herself and I know she heard my thoughts.

Come on, Amelia! I'm too old for this! I don't like crawling among worms and slime and sludge! But Amelia plunges forward, under a bush and out the other side. A small maple tree hangs over the lip of the river with a narrow branch that Amelia grabs with both hands. Then she picks up her feet and dangles over the water just inches below. I'm going to regret this tomorrow when my muscles will surely be complaining. But it's her body now, not mine.

She swings from side to side, bouncing her feet off the shore, until she spots something among the trees on the other side of the path and moves away from the water. In only seconds, she's on the back of a huge tree taken down by a storm probably a generation ago. Amelia drops down onto her stomach for a tree-hug and lies in blissful tree-love with her cheek pressed against the rough bark. I struggle against her mental iron grip and lose, and feel sorry for Sean and Molly who are not nearly so infatuated with this tree as Amelia is. *Come on, Amelia! Let me come back!*

We finally move on and eventually get to the end of the path, near the truck. I get my hopes up that Amelia, who is still not receding at all, will go willingly but she wanders nonchalantly closer to the river. Nearer and nearer, until she is at the foot of a huge old oak that fell into the river, probably after last year's ice storm. It creates a bridge now that only reaches half way across the river. Amelia puts one foot and then the other on the trunk. She balances near the roots of the tree, still on the bank, and then out we go, along the spine of the tree with the river's current swirling inches away.

Amelia is as comfortable as a mountain goat on this tree, but I'm terrified as I look down into the dark water. I have no idea how deep it is. Amelia turns around to smirk at Sean and Molly, high and dry on the shore, and I catch a barely hidden smile on Molly's face. I think she's enjoying this!

Amelia moves as close to the top of the tree as possible, to the part that's nearest the center of the river. The part that is only now about 8 inches across and bumping a little bit with the weight of the water flowing against it. *Amelia! Please go back.* But Amelia does not go back. Instead she lowers her butt to her heels and watches the patterns where the dark, swirling river water meets the black, rotting roughness of the oak. Then she simply leaves.

Gone, like a dream when the morning alarm rings. *Damn you, Amelia!*

Gingerly, I turn my head to find Molly and Sean, still safe on the shore. I, however, am not safe. I don't have Amelia's physical abilities, her equilibrium, or her enthusiasm. How the hell am I supposed to get back to shore?

"Help!" I call to my friends.

"Help what?" Sean laughs. "Looks like you have a problem!"

"This isn't funny! I can't get back!"

"You'll have to!" Sean calls. "We can't come and get you!"

Damn, damn, damn! Slowly, and feeling like an old toad, I sidestep, one tiny motion at a time, until I have moved myself to the barrel-sized bottom of the big tree and onto the swampy, but solid, shore.

"We're going home!" I snort. I have had enough fun.

But later a guide comes in. There is no rest from them today.

"She must listen to what feels right and do the right thing! No busywork! That busywork is for later! She is on a different path now. 'Amelia of the Path' has shown her new paths and possibilities, but cannot walk them for her! She must find her own and walk them fearlessly. Get off the old path. Amelia is childlike – be like a child!"

Then another shift, like a cloud drifting beneath the sun, and my energy drains. I feel a drop in Molly's energy as well and her face alters, as mine must when I am not myself. Molly's expression moves from welcome, to wariness.

"Children inside her scream in the silence," an unnatural, sticky voice nearly whispers. "They exist trapped in their silence as she digs to uncover them. Only she can expose their pain and release it. She must be childlike to express it. The little ones are trapped and waiting. When they are released, they will be gone. Ruby Red is in a China doll. Find her. Repair the damage to get her back. You must get through the keeper. Ruby Red is protected and isolated."

The Worlds Within

Guides and personalities move through me easily and expect that Molly, Sean and I, and even the girls, will just deal with it. But it gets old and we tire of it. I am worn out, these last days of October, and, once again, work is taking a toll on me. And yet work seems mundane and trivial compared to the incredible events that occur within me. This is an unsettled time and it's not just the coming of winter, but the sense that my old life is blowing away like leaves from the trees.

A guide comes in during my appointment with Dr. Allen. It takes over as I rest in the background. I've heard their spiel before. My entire foundation is being rebuilt. I have much internal work to do. I get tangled in busywork and I don't remember my treasures. I need to give up my previous belief system and claim what the alters and guides are giving me.

Then she warns that this is a dangerous time in the healing process. I have no new tools yet, and the old tools don't work. Trying to return to old behaviors makes me even more weak and vulnerable. It's dangerous to try to use the old, familiar ways, because when they don't work, it's tempting to rely on other means like medication and alcohol to ease the pain.

Dr. Allen surprises me by recommending that I take more time off work because I am regressing. I'm not eating again or sleeping through the night. He gives me paperwork to turn in at work for disability benefits. On one hand, I'm relieved, because I feel depleted and flat, and putting up a brave front is very hard; but, on the other hand, will I ever be able to take care of myself? Being relieved of the burden of work feels good – and bad – and both are stressful.

The guides continue to bombard us with information as I hang out at Sean and Molly's house on this cold Thursday. It's

Halloween night and the girls are at the apartment for trick-or-treating and to pass out candy.

Molly takes this opportunity to ask once more about the guides. Who are they and what is their purpose?

"Our knowledge is not of your world. You can only understand our words based on your personal experience, knowledge and awareness. We cannot break through your belief in your world of busywork and old habits. You must ask to be shown the way. We bring understanding to anyone who asks to find their own bridge, but we cannot teach those who do not ask.

"A powerful force runs through everything. Through this world and beyond, but many are blinded by the outside world. She is learning to truly 'see.' This power is always there, the trick is to put it into a form that others can understand. What we teach is like sunshine, there for all who want it. She will help others to awaken, learn and understand, but then they will take their own journeys. If they care enough to see where this Light comes from, they will be changed. Her power will be used for healing. She will face rejection, but she will succeed."

I need to stop now, to rest, gather my thoughts, and rebuild my beliefs. The busywork can wait now that I'm not working. I can open safely now without a time clock or censorship. But I can't process tonight. I'm spent.

Liza

We came with help and hope. We came for strength and healing. We pushed, we enlightened, we let her see beyond the veil. Everything, all of it, was specifically arranged for her. It was not done to her, however ... it was done by her. She asked for peace and the release of love, for the understanding of her soul, for the separation from the world. She asked and she allowed and she found the strength to hear us. Yes, there was struggle, but it was the struggle between the truth and lies. Lies that had existed for many years and had held her captive. She knew there was more... that she was more. Do not think that we were cruel or uncaring. We were drawn to her by the yearning of her wounded heart. We are, in truth, a part of her and accessed simply because she was willing to let go and allow us to be revealed.

You are no different. You are no less deserving of happiness, joy and love. The question is, are you willing to receive it?

Jayd

It may seem that Rebecca's liberation from the past came at a price, and that's true. But the price she paid, in the end, made the whole experience priceless. Without the challenge, the great lessons of Being would never have been learned. Within the struggle came answers, growth, awareness, enlightenment, love and, finally, the peace she craved.

Saying Good-Bye

The fog returns and Depression Girl rises once more as November enters cold and cloudy. No more work for now, and that's a very good thing. I can't function again and it's all caving in on me. I thought I was handling it so well, but juggling my "busywork," and my emotional and physical recovery, has beaten me down again.

As the days pass, I now question everything I thought I knew about myself and my life. Alters and guides push and push so that I cannot fall back into old ways. I think the psychiatrist I still see twice a week should be more help, but he offers no suggestions. He only listens as I dutifully describe my daily life and the alters and guides within it. He gives me little feedback and no clues to the darkness in my mind. Sean and Molly do the work and have the burden of care for me. My personalities come out occasionally during my sessions, but it's usually to communicate something to me. They know that by speaking with others, they are expressing to me.

The divorce will be final soon. My mind drifts too often lately to thoughts of Thom, and I fight thick hopelessness. Then, I give in. See? I'm not struggling anymore, please end this pain. And what have I been fighting all this time? An image created for me by others. Negative beliefs, attitudes, expectations, experiences, lessons. They poison mind and soul, numb the spirit, and quiet the voice within; and the image feeds upon the poison, and grows and strengthens. So much nourishment for it - so little for the soul, until you do not know what is reality and what is illusion. A little at a time. Pain disguised as love. Struggling has only strengthened it. And now that I see that, I hope it's over. I want to move on.

Sean and Molly decide a walk would help us all, so we go to the park. I doubt we'll see Amelia here today, considering how depleted I am. I feel bad for my friends, whose lives are now so tangled up in the mess that is my life. I wouldn't blame them for backing away, but at the same time, I could not go on without them. They say they have nothing else going on anyway, and they've learned so much through this. So, here we are together, caught in a crop circle, transcending logic or denial, and we can't leave until the puzzle is solved.

We tread the packed brown earth of the familiar trail. The leaves have fallen and the trees are quiet. There is none of the lushness that nurtured Amelia. No leaves to whisper to her and no songbirds to call the way. There is silence except for our padding footsteps and the push of the river over rocks and fallen trees.

"She doesn't believe all that we have said," confides a voice in the quiet. "She always doubts us. She sees with eyes of the external world. She doesn't understand the potential. This is great change and upheaval, and she believes only what her five senses tell her. She does not yet appreciate that she walks between two worlds. She can be of both worlds."

Then she stops and looks at Sean and Molly.

"There is no one better to help her than you. But you can help or delay. You could do great damage to her and so you are being pushed as well. You must understand that she has lost her old life and you are her support. But if you choose not to be involved, a China doll will be on the shelf. There will be none of our world in her. How much do you give and how much do you give up? And how much are you willing to get?"

The guide speaks to my fears about how much my friends can handle, but Sean and Molly have also gained. They sacrifice, but they learn along with me. And the guides are right, I do see progress and that I have lived my life in fear, feeling powerless and dominated. I tried to please others and that only produced unhappiness for everyone.

We take a break on a bench overlooking a bend in the river. The breeze feels good and the guide is gone. A comforting peace surrounds the three of us and it's nice to just sit quietly. The guide, and this quiet moment, have created a bond between us even stronger than before. Then Amelia eases in as she can't resist the power of the park and the protection of the trees, but her vitality is low, like my own.

"I have to go. I don't want to leave you, but I have to go back."

Molly and Sean move protectively closer as my chest constricts at this surprise and my eyes fill with tears. I'm not sure if they're mine or Amelia's.

"I'm sad to go. I love it here." Amelia sighs, as she soaks up her final moments. She is such a beautiful spirit. I love her. I know Sean and Molly love her, too. Damn it! Damn it! Why is this taking me by surprise and hurting so badly? And why do I care? She is not real! These alters are not me! They are fiction, created in a lonely child's mind years ago. I should be happy that I'm healing…but right now my heart is breaking. I want to hold this little tree urchin and keep her safe? *Amelia, you do not exist and yet I cannot let you leave me.*

Tears flow as Amelia says good-bye, soon to be alone once more. Except now she *knows* that she's alone. How cruel to teach her of love and send her back into exile. Then, as I should expect, she gives us a smile.

"You won't forget me, because every time you come to the park, I'll be here. I'll be inside you. I'll be right here inside you."

We ride in silence back to the house. This day has gone on for weeks and I am drained.

After a quick dinner, a guide comes in once more.

"Amelia is crying at her tree, but she will soon forget. Amelia had lessons to learn about limitations and love; and about restrictions and freedom; and about boundaries."

She isn't real! She is fantasy!

"What is reality?" the guide responds instantly to my thoughts. "What is fantasy? How can you be sure? People need a common reality so they don't have to start over each morning. Without that, life would only be a dream. But don't judge reality. Amelia's rules and lessons are different from Ruby Red's. The Little Ones live in different places with different rules. Can you tell them they don't exist? Can you create their reality?"

The guides are right. I can't define reality. Amelia is real, at least to us, and I must remember what she gave us.

Lessons from Amelia of the Path:

Look for new paths.
There are many paths and each has something wonderful.
The best path isn't always the one everyone else is on.
Listen to the trees and the water - they whisper, sing and speak to you.
The wind and water can speak only when they meet with an obstacle.
Run and play and explore and watch and listen and feel and grow.
Appreciate the path you're on.
Wondrous treasures are hidden behind what you thought you knew.
Freedom is a state of mind.
Getting dirty is okay and makes you feel good.
Yap, yap, yap.

I miss her. And I'll never go to the park again without thinking of her. I won't forget her or her lessons. *I have written them down, Amelia, for you.* Charming, cajoling, persistent, expansive, determined, delightful, playful, trusting Amelia of the Path.

Moving On

The guides say fighting change will only make it more difficult and add more obstacles. I must honor the lessons of Amelia and get off the old path. Divorce is just another path. Things are getting better, with less pain. There is a joyous event coming.

The alters have backed off into this third week of November. Maybe my mind is too full. Even though I'm still off work, I have plenty to think about. Today is the final court date for the divorce. But first, I meet Lee at the recognition luncheon at the county school district offices. She was one of four students asked to share her experiences from last June's program at the university. She is confident, poised and eloquent, and I am so proud of her. It's hard not to think of Thom as I watch her captivate the many school administrators and teachers in the audience. *We did well with our girls, Thom. They are magnificent. And now I leave the luncheon so I can officially end the life that you and I shared.*

I'm to return to work next week, so Dr. Allen spoke at my office today to help ease fears that I'm a danger there, although he does admit that some disruption is possible. Alma refused to attend, but Marcia spoke plainly for them both. They want me out of the department. They think I am a threat somehow. But, everyone else supports me and I will go back when it's time.

The next day is my last session with Dr. Allen before Thanksgiving. The divorce is final and I'm dealing with that now, but the multiple personalities go on and on. I try to be positive, and it's been an incredible experience, but it's hard and even though I don't want my old life, I would like to claim my new one.

Today the doctor asks about my relationship with my mother. I tell him I have no issues with her except that she could have shared her feelings more, and I wish she was healthier. Headaches were a constant torment for her, and consequently for us all.

170

As the years passed, the headaches got worse. Many holidays, birthdays and family gatherings were missed or spoiled because of headaches. If Mom couldn't attend, none of us were allowed to go. If we did go when she had a headache, she would often take pain medication and sleep in the car.

I tell the doctor about all the surgeries, drugs, hypnotherapy, biofeedback, kinesiology, and acupuncture she endured, and about her many stays at several hospitals. Dad complained about money spent on failed treatments and medication and "quack" doctors and their inability to find anything wrong. Through the years her problems worsened. Phlebitis required weekly blood tests. Blood thinners joined the beta blockers and narcotics she was already taking for pain. She fell often, or hurt herself in other ways. She was always bruised. Everyone felt sorry for her. I don't remember a time when she was well.

As I recite all this to Dr. Allen, he settles more comfortably into his high-backed leather chair. He always listens calmly, not responding except for the occasional question. Today, though, he has more to say.

"I believe your mother has somatic disorder. It's a diagnosis I specialize in, but the success rate for curing it is almost zero. A person with this disorder creates illness to get attention. Sometimes they 'accidentally' hurt themselves. It serves a purpose in your mother's life. No mentally healthy person would go through what she has suffered most of her life. Your mother will never be well because she doesn't want to be."

Oh, those dominos again. Mom said her headaches began right after she married Dad, when she was 19 years old. They got worse through the years, I suspect as he became more controlling. But she rarely confronted him about anything. She simply set her jaw, crossed her arms and refused to speak. She wouldn't argue or even express an opinion with him. She did, however, tell him everything that Rene', Devon and I did, knowing there would be consequences. Yet she was never around for those consequences.

Except once. I remember the day Dad used the willow switch on me that Mom stood just feet away, holding Rene's hand... watching! And she did nothing.

I am speechless as my session with Dr. Allen ends. I thought I had one parent to count on. How could I have been so blind? Why didn't I see it before?

"You knew nothing else. Your childhood was unhealthy. You endured stress that was equivalent to a war zone." the doctor says, as I walk out the door. "There was nothing you could have done."

This was a huge revelation and for two days after my doctor's visit I've lived with the misery of this information. Thanksgiving was yesterday, but is not even a memory. Tonight, I am with Sean and Molly, trying to understand. I'm grateful for the guide who comes through. It's a reprieve from the overwhelming pain... for a minute.

"Think of death," she says, "For a small child, watching your father come at you with a weapon would be like looking into the eyes of death. Think of all the feelings that would go with that, knowing your life is in someone's hands and there is no escape. You think that event was not enough to cause the alters. You are wrong."

Innocence loses to pain, and the truth of a hard life with a hard man and a self-obsessed mother. My mind says we're being dramatic, but my heart knows it's true.

Later, somehow alone in the apartment, I methodically strip all the leaves off my plants, like I have been stripped of childhood. I can't help myself. It just seems right. Then I pick up the leaves, one by one, and toss them out the door.

Into The Future

The next night a guide comes in as usual, but I'm in no mood for analysis. I've had enough of that lately. But, of course, I might as well try to stop the wind.

"It is time to use new tools. The old places are no more. Those people, her parents, no longer determine her future."

"She thinks she should have done something as a child to change all this." Molly says.

"No, there was no way to change the outcome. She did not contribute to her mother's illness in any way she could have controlled at the time. There was nothing a child could do, and mental illness cannot take care of itself."

"Did her father contribute to her mom's illness?" Molly continues.

"Theirs was a complicated relationship. Neither knew they had a problem. Consider that her mother was competing for her father's attention and shut the children out. The parents created the close relationship between their children that exists to this day. They created too much responsibility for children. She could not heal without this truth about her mother. She can't rebuild her life on false assumptions. The new life must be built upon truth, love, understanding, compassion, and sympathy. All that a human being deserves."

On the last day of November, Peter Pan comes to play with Sean and Ann while Elizabeth and Lee visit their father. Within Peter, behind forts of pillows and blankets, throwing and dodging paper wads and stuffed bears and other soft toys until bedtime, I am happier.

I am released to return to work again on Monday. I sincerely hope a weight has been lifted now and the worst is over. So much has happened these last months to change me. "You can't see it and still live in it," the guides keeping telling us. Alters and guides have left no dark corners unexplored. Cobwebs are swept, windows wiped clean and nothing is left beneath the rug. They've changed my life; expanded my view; given me myself. They've given me permission, and freedom, to feel and express my emotions. This is beyond anything I could have done for myself. They have pried loose the demons of my past, exposed them, and they have melted away. Anger has no more power. It's simply fear in disguise. And others will carry their own burdens now. I've learned so much. I look forward to the future again. I have hope.

The night before I return to work, Celeste surprises us with her return. "When her light nearly went out in June, we had to make ourselves known to her. We chose this form for your comfort. The door was easy to open with her. We don't want control, we want everything she wants for herself. She must always have busywork; that is irrelevant. Her new path will be different. Now she must learn to trust and nurture herself. She can now hear the voices within her heart that bring a new life."

"We're still not clear about something." Molly says. "Is all this, with the guides, about being psychic?"

"We do not care for that term. Everyone is 'psychic,' but tuned in at different levels and for different reasons. Everyone has their purpose and their place in the world. Yes, she receives knowledge from us. Guidance we give her, however, will affect others. The spark we have lit must not be allowed to go out."

Liza and Curly Words

In mid-December, I recline on pillows piled on the floor in front of the blazing fireplace at Sean and Molly's while Sean relaxes on the couch. I hear Molly's and the girls' voices in another room. I gaze up to the highest peak of the cathedral ceiling, then down to the fireplace beneath the mantle, but I am not myself and my thoughts twist inside my head. The words in my mind "curl," and my tongue shifts without permission. I try to talk to Sean, but the first two attempts come out garbled. I pause and try once more to say something out loud.

"Oi've got cuhly wuds in my 'ead." Huh? One more time, I try to explain. "Oi don' know wut's up, but moi wuds ain't straight." *What the hell?!?*

"Who are you?" Sean asks. "Have you got a name?"

"Of course Oi've got a nayme!" she laughs. "It's Loiza!!"

"Liza?" says Sean. "Well, Liza, what can we do for you?"

But, as quickly as it began, it's over. Liza is gone, but she leaves me with an image. She's young and thin with long, blond hair hanging loose with wispy bangs that give way to a soft cut around her ears. And huge, sparkling eyes. She feels carefree and incorrigible. Free and funky and feisty.

Two days later, I travel away from the mystery and back into reality. It all seems to have caught up with me and tonight requires total truth. I've repressed my emotions for too long. I am angry about the abuse and neglect. The control and the selfishness. Dr. Allen said my parents should not have had children. Can I, should I, place blame? Will it change anything? The alters and guides torment me until I relive every moment. Why can't they just let us be?

Then, for the next few days, Liza returns and my mood swings the other way. She is a happy break from the angst and pain, and already one of the girls' favorites. She is interested in everything they say so they cozy up and enjoy her presence and her curly words. Liza is real. Not a piece of me, or an obvious lesson to be learned. She's honest and natural and fun. She is the moment. Because of her "curly words," the girls ask where she's from.

"Where are *you* from?!" she answers with a wink. She means their essence, of course. Their selfness. "Why is moi existence any more improbable than yer own?"

She's right. Where *is* our sense of self born? Where does that part of us exist that is so changeable, and altered, in the course of our lives?

Freedom For Our Friends

Thom picks up the girls from the apartment this afternoon to spend the night; one of the few overnight visits since the divorce. The apartment is unbearable without them, though, and I wonder how they're getting along. I pick up a book, trying to enjoy the solitude, but I only get through a couple pages before words tumble together. After I've read the same sentence three times, I pick up the phone. Then I put the receiver back.

Don't do it! I warn myself. *Leave them alone.*

We've given Molly and Sean a night and half a day of freedom, but they deserve much more. I pick up the phone again and listen to the dial tone.

"Damn you!" I curse myself for being so weak and needy, but I dial anyway. I need the warmth of my friends' house and the cheer of their multitudes of Christmas decorations.

"Come on out!" Molly invites. Did I catch an edge to her voice? "We're just sitting around watching movies. You might as well join us. Better than being alone." It's a zillion times better than being alone and I hate my selfishness.

A Christmas movie, one of Sean's favorites, is playing as I settle into a corner of the leather couch, hoping not to be intrusive and pleading internally for a night off. I lose my thoughts into the glowing Christmas tree, and they wind around ornaments and spin with the marquee lights. Around and around, fitting nicely with the subtle strains of *Silent Night* that repeat themselves in my brain. Over and over and over until I am mentally out of the way and our quiet evening is interrupted as always. My mind snaps back to attention but it's too late.

"We have some ripping out to do that will hurt. Rebecca can't see what we're doing, and feels she's stuck." My voice sounds irritated and fussy and my friends dutifully pull their attention away from the movie. Ann, lounging on a body pillow on the floor, doesn't even notice. It's old news after all this time.

The voice whines, "She messes things up. She thinks she can do this by herself; that she doesn't need us. She's afraid of us, and doesn't like us. We'll give her exactly what she needs. She hurts and she's scared and she's tired. She doesn't want you involved. She wants to take care of this herself. Talk to the Others. They will help you."

Then she focuses on Molly and Sean. "You help her heal, when you tell her she didn't cause the pain. When you make her see what they did, and ask what she did to deserve it. Make her stop protecting and justifying. Feelings are attached to her wounds! Make her see the wounds! The wounds must be opened and cleaned and healed. She is safe to bleed – and to heal."

In my mind, I squirm and fumble like an animal trapped in a gunny sack, so sorry I drove here. The movie is spoiled now, and there is nothing for my friends to say once the alter recedes. They've heard it and heard it and heard it.

"We've got to go to town," Molly tells Sean. "We've got some things to pick up."

I feel chastised, and with good reason. I have to stop this. I have to find some way to control it. My friends should not have to put up with me yet again.

"Going with us, Ann?" Molly calls.

Ann rolls over, confused at the underlying tension. "Sure," she says as she stretches and bounces to her feet.

"We'll be back soon." Molly at least gives me that as the three of them find their coats and she jingles the car keys. Within seconds they're pulling out of the driveway.

I can't stand it anymore. I resent being the "vessel." I'm done with it. I'm done with it for my friends. I leave a note of thanks and drive home.

I realize, curled in my bed at midnight, that I am the only person who can heal any damage I feel has been done to me. My parents are not the same people who controlled my childhood, and made mistakes as parents do. They can't fix anything for me. I must make my own peace with it. A vision enters my mind and I must write it. I must make it real and keep it for later. For the child I was then, and the woman I am now. This requires no alter and no guide. This is me, seeing it differently, making it real, and changing the past:

I carry her awkwardly out of the sun, careful not to touch the backs of her legs. The wounds are fresh. She makes no sound as I lay her on her stomach on the couch in the cool, shadowy living room. As I kneel beside her, damp gauzy white fabric appears in my hands, and I tenderly apply it to the willow switch's red streaks.

She does not move and I cannot even hear her breath. Her eyes open but there is no expression, no indication of pain, no knowledge of what just happened. I touch a warm, smooth cheek with the back of my hand, just to let her know I am here.

Barely whispering, I say she will be okay, that I will take care of her, that she did not deserve this beating, and I will stay with her and protect her and love her. I kiss her face and smooth the curls near her ear. I promise that no one will hurt her again. She turns her face to the back of the couch and I am glad because at least she moved. I stroke her back and arms and hair, telling her over and over that I will not leave her.

Our parents enter the room, but do not step into our safe space, and I confront them and challenge their choices and their behavior. My fury brings tears that I can now cry for both of us. The rage and anguish and pain, gathered through time. I expel it all, expressing everything the limp little body on the couch cannot, until my heart is cleansed and my mind satisfied.

*Then I turn to her and tell her what they could not.
I offer assurances of comfort and healing. I grant her grace
and purity as I find the treasures within her and offer
her each one, cleansed with tears and returned with love.
And, for me, she smiles.*

Christmas Miracles

The Christmas season brings hope and high spirits and a sense of forgiveness, and, after a few days apart, the girls are ready to spend time with Ann, and Molly is thankfully prepared to be of service once more. As we spend the evening with them, it's business as usual.

"You are both here to learn," a guide tells Sean and Molly. "What you learn depends on you. The transformation has begun. There will soon be new parts to meet. You must be there to meet them and to see them as treasures, and all three of you will gain."

We've established our pattern in the evenings these recent snowy days before Christmas. We work, we eat, we wait for a guide. But finally the girls are out of school on Christmas break and busy with holiday plans. What a relief to rest and look forward to a new year, but it's our first Christmas without Thom. Of course, the girls will split the day between us, but time spent with him means alone time for me. I won't intrude on my friends' Christmas plans with their families. I'll be just fine, the girls and I will make new traditions, and I will wish Thom a happy new life.

Tonight a soft snow falls in the twilight, and the giant Christmas tree sparkles in the center of Sean and Molly's living room, reaching at least 10 feet toward the peak of the cathedral ceiling. There are already presents beneath it, and the radio blasts rock and roll Christmas songs from two huge speakers in the corner. It's festive here, but it always is. They love Christmas and they're generous with us. There is plenty to eat, lots of presents, and lots of love and laughter. The girls hide in Ann's room to wrap presents and tell secrets, and Molly and Sean and I don't have to wait long before I fade and a voice speaks softly through me.

"Help us! You must greet the new ones. We have been waiting. We could not exist in the sadness and have waited for her to accept us. There is now comfort, nurturing, help, and freedom. The bridge now nestles in a lush setting. Before, there was no landscape. Now it is green, fresh, vibrant and beautiful with a waterfall behind it. She can't exist without water. Tell her to go to the bridge. See it, feel it. It flows from all her yesterdays into all her tomorrows. The source of the waterfall is our Source."

As usual, Molly is scribbling notes and trying to make sense of the guide's imagery. Sean is on his side on the floor with his head propped in the curve of his elbow. His eyes are closed, but that doesn't mean he's sleeping.

Then the guide looks at Molly and then Sean. "There is more. We would have you walk this bridge with her. Through you, the river began to flow. You've given back all that was taken. Yet your journey is not over. You cannot give love without getting it in return. You will find your own miracles and treasures. What you have done will come back to you."

On Christmas Eve, we play in the holiday snow globe that is our friends' home. Music, lights on the tree, unwrapping presents and eating fresh popcorn. Christmas movies and a warm fire. Snow drifting lightly outside the window. Just the six of us. It's nearly midnight when we leave, grateful and happy to have them in our lives.

Lee and Elizabeth will spend Christmas afternoon with their dad and it casts a shadow over my Christmas morning. There are only a few presents beneath the little tree in the living room of our apartment, the floor is cold, and the girls pretend not to hear the hollow clink of the holiday. It isn't home. I wistfully remember last year in our living room with me snuggled against Thom in the corner of the plush sectional, a toasty fire in the stone fireplace, and the dog nosing through the many presents to find his treats. Lee passes out gifts and they accumulate around us… and, god, what am I doing! Shake it off! It's done. It's over. Get used to it.

Elizabeth snuggles with me on the daybed as Lee opens the big box with her name on it. It's a down comforter to cover her at night in the cold bedroom. She can't quite hide her disappointment with the practical gift, and obligingly drapes it around her shoulders. Damn. I thought she'd like it, but it just goes bust on an already unsatisfying day. Elizabeth and I open our gifts and make a big deal over them. We're trying so hard.

But then Lee says, "This is awesome!" She's almost disappeared into the feather tick and I see her eyes sparkling in the center. "This is sooooo warm! Ooohhh!!" I laugh at her, and the room is warmer now as Elizabeth relaxes against me with her presents. I am grateful to be here with my kids, and thankful to them for being so wonderful. Happy to be healthier and to have made it this far. It's a good day after all.

An Interview With A Guide

I want to know if we can interact with the guides instead of just listening like obedient children, so a couple days after Christmas I compile some questions. I hope the guides will come through if we ask for them.

"Can we call in a guide?" Molly asks. I feel silly, sitting here like a ventriloquist's dummy, but when they come through, it isn't like that. It feels right and natural.

"We are here," a guide answers.

"Is it okay to talk to you and ask questions?"

"We are here for guidance. We are here for the asking."

"Can Rebecca communicate with you through writing?"

"It is a way to ask."

"Okay, then," Molly continues. "And now we would like to ask a couple questions. First, what exactly is the 'wisdom?'"

"The wisdom flows through all things living. It is the life force, the source, the means to change... the energy. Without the energy, there is no growth. The energy is like water. It flows down the easiest path. Removing obstacles allows for greater force."

"Are there rules for using the energy?"

"Use it wisely and enjoy it. Do not try to control or manipulate it. Build no more dams. Carry no more burdens. A river creates its own path. Let it flow. Energy seeks expression. It only requires silence and intent."

"Why has the energy chosen to express through Rebecca?"

"The energy will not be denied. It was meant for her. But she must learn not to drown in it. Intent is crucial. Everyone has the ability to give and receive the energy. You can see the flow between you now. Work with it. You may ask for it, and you will be given it when you are open to receive. There is much to gain in the wisdom, but it will not compete with busywork."

"How will this change her life? And will it affect others?"

"Opening the door, allowing the energy and being the bridge is her life. Others change of their own accord. She lights the way; they decide whether to seek. They will be drawn to her according to their need. Play the song and they will hear it. It is not her concern if they do not listen. Their journey does not concern her. She is to shine the light."

The questions are answered. The guide shifts and speaks directly to Molly and Sean.

"The real journey now begins for both of you. The river has caught up to events in *your* lives. You need her energy and it will be there for you. It will soon be your turn to grow and change. We can teach you what you need to know. There will be more to come for both of you."

Happy New Year

The new year has begun. But not just a new year, a new attitude. A new life. I'm open today, and receptive, and belong more to there than to here. The alters bring healing, the guides bring truth. I exist in some hazy dimension between my physical world, and my alters and guides. I need them. I'm not complete anymore without them.

"Molly, please talk to the guides for me," I request. "Ask them what has come to life inside me, because I feel different. I want to know what it means. I want to keep this feeling. I need to know if I can rely on it."

Their answer comes immediately.

"You have opened the door to the other world. You cannot bring it here with you yet, but your soul knows, and it is from your soul that the light shines. As you grow, more of the light will shine through. You have touched your inner power. Your inner light will now illuminate your outer world. Its value and power increase when it is shared with others.

"Life doesn't just happen. It responds to your thoughts and feelings. Positive brings positive. Build a happy, productive, joyful life. Be glorious. Be wonderful. You have a new foundation, and it is strong and solid with no flaws. But the structure is not complete. It will be created between now and summer."

When the guides finish and I settle back into my body, Sean and Molly say I should stop fighting. I wish I could. I wish I could give myself completely to this new way of life, but I can't forget that I have to work and take care of the girls. No guide will pay my bills.

I've decided to find a house to buy for the girls and me. It's time for stability. I owe them that. Then we can take the dog from Thom, who doesn't want him anyway, and we can finally be home. I'll do my best to make that dream come true for them.

186

I return to work the next day and the girls are in school and we've settled in at Sean and Molly's for dinner and updates on our day. The girls run off to Ann's room, and I'm content to just watch a movie and relax. Then, of course, an alter.

"She knows who I am! She shouldn't try to keep me out! She knows why I'm angry! I'm mad at *them*! They're mean! They hurt us. They hurt all of us. We left them a long time ago. Then there was nobody to tell us what to do. We just want someone to play with!"

Then they recognize him.

"Peter Pan, why have you come?" Molly asks. We haven't seen him in a month, and never like this. There is no trace of the bravado or the fun. He's petulant and anxious tonight.

"Because they hurt us!"

"They hurt you?"

"Yes! And they never played! I hate them! They only know how to do their big people stupid stuff. They only care about themselves. They don't know how to play. They don't want anyone to play. They couldn't make me cry. They could never catch me again. They caught me once but never again."

The broken sentences fade away, but leave the familiar pain. This pain that runs through everything, the center of all of it. Water Girl's fear of being touched. Amelia's craving of nature and freedom. Peter Pan's aggression and need to play. None of these alters would have existed without that pain. They came to meet me, to acknowledge and share their feelings. They just wanted someone to talk to and to shed the tears that were not allowed to fall.

And now Peter is gone, but, sadly, still holding the pain.

Liza

Time appears to pass quickly in your world. To your eyes, change comes and you react. You feel you are at the mercy of time and circumstance, and so your awareness remains within your mind and body. You are so entrenched within your own imaginings that you cannot see beyond them. Your awareness, however, is not contained within your body, your mind, or even your heart. It is greater than that and inclusive of all things.

If you could only see that you are not inside. All is within you. Your bridge is your escape from your limited perspective. When you find the bridge, you realize that there is no harm, no destruction, no pain that is not without loving intent. This may seem impossible to believe. We invite you to see differently.

Jayd

The alters were delivering their messages and returning home, one by one. Each filling its own needs and therefore hers as well. But she kept trying to expect the unexpected, filling in the blanks with what she already knew. Walking toward the bridge brought her into new territory where little was familiar, and the old ways no longer worked, but still she could not let go of what she thought she knew.

Transformation is not easy. It, by its nature, is a destructive process. But the spiral spins forever, taking us always to new levels of rebirth.

Lights In The Fountain

"Rebecca doesn't see the alters' pain as her pain," a guide's voice says. "She just wants them to heal without involving her. She must face her fears. Each alter gave her treasures. She can't be complete without them. She thought she outgrew the need to play, take different paths, be loved, be herself, and sparkle with life and color. No one outgrows that!! Each time she lets her guard down and steps into a new awareness she sheds more of the old image. To receive all things once denied her, she must accept them. A gift cannot be given if it is not received."

The voice gets stronger and more forceful.

"She must embrace all five of the Little Ones! She needs Amelia who explored new paths; Water Girl, who wanted love to replace the fear, and whose sensations connect with the flow of life; Peter Pan who teaches the joy and freedom in play; Ruby Red who is pure and radiates color; the China Doll who just wants to be real. NO ONE OUTGROWS THESE! They have come home. All parts of the whole together again. She must return the treasures to each of them to make their lights glow. They have survived in the tiny bit of water remaining in the center of her, suspended in time, waiting for just this moment.

"Help her to stay in the moment. She must not put the alters and feelings away now. She must believe and accept herself as she is. We came to unfold aspects of her personality that were given at birth. They were meant to blossom as she grew and experienced and learned. They are her gifts, her treasures. But they weren't allowed to grow. They must now be recognized, drawn out, nurtured, and appreciated.

"The China Doll doesn't play or talk. She doesn't join in. She stands at the edge like a shadow. She needs her treasures. She wants to play, but she doesn't have life inside."

I see a picture in my mind of a lost little girl, afraid to join in, afraid not to. Not sure where to go or what to do. Afraid of making a mistake. My heart swells with understanding. I know those feelings. I remember. Now I see all the Little Ones gathered near the big white house, the full porch facing the setting sun. I see them connected and communicating. Except for her. Her face is lifeless and her eyes hopeless. She waits at the edge to be told what to do.

"There are Others that wait near her. The guides. They see the light around her. They can tell you what she needs. She must accept herself before she can join the rest. She must feel first. She must heal first.

"She put herself away, destroyed her essence, to be what she isn't. She denied and despised those parts of herself, but it all must be accepted now. The denied parts became pieces and must come back together. She became like her parents so she could be seen by them and accepted. She traded life for darkness. Stuck in a little box of rules."

I think about them later, in my bed in the apartment. I think about the parts they say I put away. How can that be, though? I've lived a full life, a happy life for the most part. My parents didn't keep me in a cage, for god's sake. I did play and travel and have friends. But something niggles inside me. Was I happy? I thought so at the time, but I was so clueless as a kid. I lived an unexamined life, like most people, I think. But it seems I have to scour every bit of it now. Why make me review memories that are pointless if I can't change them? I've been pushed and dragged and for what? If it's my mind, my imagination, and my lifetime fueling all this, I hope I'm smart enough to give myself a happy ending.

It's now the first week of January and I've given up any control I thought I had of the alters at work. Liza has entered the building. I can only ride along and hope for the best. There are too many social contacts here for her to resist. Today she jokes and mingles and chats and does everything but work. Liza doesn't just socialize, she owns the place. She introduces herself all around and then marches into the director's office.

"Moi name is Loiza," she says, sticking out her hand, "It's good ta meetcha!" I'm getting fired for sure. But I see a smile form on the director's weathered face. His hand wraps around mine, big and warm and gentle.

"Liza," he says, "it's nice to meet you. But I have to tell you that we have work to do here and we take it very seriously. If you're going to be here, you have to do what you're getting paid to do. I don't expect any problems."

"And there won't be any!" Liza fires back. "No problem, Jim!"

So, we go back into the spotlight and to my cubicle to work until Liza decides she's had enough.

It's a long week. I'm stressed and on guard all the time as I move from one way of being to another. I'm under the microscope every day at work, constantly watched and gossiped about and why not? I'd do the same thing, not knowing how challenging it is. It's exhausting to work with all this energy running through me.

Every day after work, another and another and another. They don't let up and they don't let me rest. Even in my dreams there is no peace. My nights are restless with shadows that follow me into the daylight. The alters and guides build a world I can't escape. They are real. I am not. I am real. They are not. But still the work goes on and life unfolds and I try to hold it all together. Then I attempt to claim it and believe it's part of me and all for some higher good, but it doesn't fit into the world I've known. It's made of pixie dust and shadows and painful recollections of the worst days. Why don't the alters bring memories of fun and laughter and love? There was that as well. My family played and we enjoyed our good times. Where is that in the world in my mind? They are ripping me apart.

"She must connect the five lights within her when the time comes," a guide tells Sean and Molly tonight.

"Are they happy?" Molly wonders.

"Yes, but scared. They know they will be one when they join together, but they are not a part of her. We have changed her and prepared her for them, but merging does not mean they become part of her."

"What are they doing when they merge then?" Molly asks. "What happens to them?"

"They are the energy in her heart. As she opens they will come to her. She must tell them she needs them, but she is afraid of what they will do to her. Her truth is before her. She has to be herself and she is afraid."

"How do they merge?" Molly asks. "How do the 'lights' come together?"

"They will unite when she accepts their feelings inside her heart and mind. But just as she did not decide to split, she cannot will them together. We will unite them for her soon. She will be whole in many ways and more true to her nature than ever before. You will see the person who would have been. They have also learned, and they will serve her well."

...And then, still, there is Liza. In the last few days, she's spoken with school secretaries, insurance reps and co-workers throughout the entire company. Her curly words wrap around them and somehow bewitch everyone who hears them. People come to my desk and ask for her! "Where's the happy girl with the English accent?"... "the Australian accent"... "the Scottish accent?"

How can I explain Liza? She's tucked inside me like the rest of them. How do I explain that I'm a little boy and a powerhouse named Lynn and a cat and a few fairies and, good god, how can I expect anyone to understand what is impossible to explain?! Liza! Why must you come out at work and force me to clean up your mess?! Why must you have an accent that attracts so much interest and attention!

"Exactly!" She tells us later in her perky, adorable, endearing way. "That's the point! Stop 'iding who you are! Stop 'olding back and repressing your love for life. Stop caring wha' people think and show 'em another way. Show 'em how to get their 'eads out of their butts and 'ave fun! Life is not serious and it's simply not as 'ard as most people make it."

Liza

We on this side of the bridge exist without a body of our own. We do not need to be anchored to the world in a temporary vessel. And neither do you in the end. The physical is a construct and a playground. In your world, you learn about cause and effect, consequences, gain and loss. It has unlimited potential to provide you with all you could desire to learn. Some of you select, in your true state, to enter the body to experience lack, and some to learn of privilege. You cannot judge, with human eyes or mind, another's path to the bridge.

But everyone, in their own time, will choose to come home. You will feel the desire of the All, and you will answer with a question. And if you ask, you will be heard. Never, ever are you not heard, or lost, or unvalued. You are love and loved.

Jayd

Five little lights within. Amelia, Ruby Red, Peter, Water Girl and the China doll. All pieces of childhood. Innocence, rebellion, sensitivity, loyalty, curiosity and potential. Honest and open and ready for life. We never lose these parts of ourselves. We never lose these qualities. We just cover them with layers of compromise, conformity and practical education. The alters returned these gifts to Rebecca in the most creative and loving way possible. They brought them to life. They let her live through them. And through their example, she could remove the years and the hard life lessons and she could be free again.

What greater act of love than to fan the spark again and bring to life these buried treasures?

Coming Home

We've found a house! A perfect house! We know it as soon as we walk through the door. The girls fan out behind me as we enter the most welcoming house the realtor has shown us in days. Newly decorated in burgundy and dark greens.

"Make an offer, Mom!" the girls prod, and I already agree. The floor plan flows from the entry into the living room, through an open dining area, and straight to the kitchen where the back door opens onto a grassy back yard that will be perfect for the dog. We'll each have our own room! I can barely take it all in before the girls drag me up the stairway to a tiny second floor with two bedrooms and another full bath. Oh, glory! The girls get their own bathroom! They're happier than I've seen them in a long time, and as I listen to them playfully argue over who gets which bedroom, I believe we can actually do this. And we've found our perfect house without help from Sean and Molly. We can do this!

After three days of torture, our wait is over. Our offer is accepted. We can't wait to get back inside, to show it to our friends, and to make it our own. I'm nervous, but proud that I can take care of us. I *will* take care of us and I know we'll be happy here. The closing is in two weeks and we can move in on the first of March. Only a few weeks away! I feel close to the girls again. I feel like an adult again.

We see our friends to tell them about the house and, of course, we can't even have one night to celebrate. When my voice changes, the girls tiptoe to the basement so we can be alone. They know the routine. We all know the routine.

"When the water came again, she had to have the bridge. So we gave her the best, strongest bridge we could build."

The little voice ages and becomes the soft, gentle rhythm of a guide's connection.

"This is good. The Little Ones are content. They were asking, restless, needing to be heard and acknowledged. They wanted to matter to someone. They have felt that now. Children should not be left crying. The children inside were trying to provide everything for themselves, but each was alone."

The guide turns toward Molly and Sean. "Now they have each other and you. But each personality remains. They are connected but still separate. One soul that has been shattered is putting itself back together."

The guides say I've changed, and I have – but by their will, not mine. I try to hold onto what they tell me and how bright the future may be and how I'll be so much better than I am now. I want to believe, but their thoughts don't get me to work in the morning and they don't keep me warm at night. They don't reassure my children or support me when I try to keep our lives on track. I hope that someday their optimistic vision comes to pass, that my world glows with good will and happiness and then all the guides and personalities can line up to say "we told you so!" In the meantime, though, they'll have to excuse a little skepticism.

Cassie

We're pushing toward the end of January and we still eat most evening meals with Sean and Molly, and stick around afterward for a while just to see who shows up. But we're so comfortable together now that it's like being home. Another night with the family. Another voice. Another unnamed entity to bring more information. Just another day.

"Those kids don't want us to come in, but we want them to like us." This new personality sends a guilty glance toward the girls, who look up to see who this one is. Those kids? My kids! Of course they don't want another new personality. They want their mom, whole and happy and focused on them, but I think they've given up hope of a normal life by now. The girls wait to see if they'll be drawn into a conversation and they sit quietly. It's unusual for them to be included and they're taking advantage of it.

"She once pushed us far away from her, but we have to express ourselves. A whole person has many parts to their personality. She has her own whole personality. Some of us developed whole personalities, too. There's more than one person here. She can keep us out, unless she wants to know about herself. Then she should move over and let us come out. It would be sad if we were left inside. She can give us a chance. We can love and play with her daughters. We use the same body, but not the same part of her brain. We're not her."

"Have you been here before?" Sean asks. "Have we met you?"

"No. I am one of the new ones. I can tell you my name. It is a very long name. Cassandra. I am Cassie."

Her tone changes when she gives us her name. She softens and seems younger. I can see her in my mind now. She's small and round and sweet, with dimples and curly dark hair that barely touches her shoulders. She's cotton candy and sweet dreams and teddy bears. I can't help myself, I like it. I like her.

"Are you one of the Others?" Molly wonders. "One of the guides?"

"I am not hooked to her life or her emotions. I'm just different. I didn't come out in the beginning while she was putting things together."

"Do you know Lynn?" Molly asks.

"Lynn knows more than everybody! She was there from the beginning. There are lots of us inside. Some got to hear and see and learn. We don't have to come out for very long. We exist inside her but if we can't talk or see then we can't 'be.' She has to move over so we can come out."

Cassie is eager for us to know her. She's ready to share any information we need. I probe internally for more depth and more attachment to me, but even though she's light and friendly, she is also rooted to my center and not about to be pushed out.

I wish Molly would keep asking questions, because even though Liza wanders through fairly regularly, it's good to have a different perspective and try to understand what they want. The sooner they get to express and leave their "lessons" with us, the sooner I can get on with my life.

"Some of us have names that we chose a long time ago. Now that the Little Ones are done, we can come out more."

"Did you come through the door?" Sean asks her.

"The door? Only the guides can open the door. But when we're out here, they can give us information that she doesn't know. They can block the information, too. Her kids have to understand we're going to be selfish with the time we have." She glances shyly at the girls, who haven't moved since the conversation started.

"We will talk to the children, though." She sends the three girls a private grin and then turns back to Sean and Molly. "We're not her at all. We're different people."

I'm getting confused by her sudden turns. It's a little hard to follow her conversation and stay on track. But I'm glad Sean and Molly keep her talking.

"I like it here!" Cassie gushes.

"We were just going to have root beer floats." Molly says. "Would you like that?"

"I don't know what that is," Cassie says. "Is it good?"

"It's one of our favorite foods!" Molly smiles and jumps up toward the kitchen. Molly's move relaxes everyone, and the girls realize this is a full-blown personality who is actually going to include them, and the mood rises a few octaves. Sean chats with Cassie while Molly and the kids get root beer floats for us all. I sit inside my head watching and waiting and trying to have no expectations of what this evening will bring. Once again I just ride along and hope for the best.

But then Cassie takes a sip of the root beer float and I feel the ice cream, cold and fluid, on my upper lip. I've never tasted root beer before, I realize. Not like this. Cool, liquid vanilla slides over my tongue and then the tingling, popping sensation of the carbonated drink and finally the earthy, pungent flavor of the root beer. My taste buds come to life and my sense of smell increases a hundred times over. I smell the tangy drink and feel the caress of the silky ice cream and then the root beer is alive in my mouth.

"Yummy," Cassie says. She doesn't bother to wipe my mouth. I don't bother her with details. We're too busy enjoying the moment and existing solely for root beer floats.

When she finally finishes and pulls herself out of the glass, I realize that it's been fun tonight. The girls are smiling and everyone has enjoyed Cassie. She's been good for us. Another one like Liza.

"This is a special place! I have to go now, but please let me come back!"

Cassie does return several times over the next week, and rests gently but firmly in my body and mind. I belong to her, and she belongs to my family and friends. They already love her and she loves them. She's filled with good will and happiness, and the girls respond eagerly to her attention. I think Cassie could charm anyone, much like Liza but without the pizzazz. She's just a sweet energy that doesn't linger nearly long enough.

Coming Undone

"She struggles with the shallow reality around her, the world of things. She must take time to go inside yet she lives in her busywork. She can make time for both, but she closes us out."

It's February now and the guides keep pounding the same message, but I don't understand where *they* are or *what* they are or how to get to *where* they are! They talk about the damned bridge and going inside and finding my parts and my pieces and my treasures. I just want to be left alone! I want to make my own choices for once in my life and move into my new house and spend time alone with my kids. I don't want to be manipulated by some mental short circuit that happened last summer. I don't want to hear about some new *place* or new *event* or new *shift*. I want to forget every bad thing that ever happened to me. Why can't I control myself, stop being the victim and get on with my life?! How can I take it seriously when everything I've ever been taught tells me it's crazy? I try to process it and "learn the lessons" and I try to understand what *they* tell me, but I can't live inside my mind. I can't let this control me. I can't go crazy. I can't!

But my thoughts are monitored and my frustration doesn't matter and the next voice I hear is chastising.

"We gave everything, and still she won't let herself feel us. She doesn't even look for what's inside. She poisons us with the lessons from this world. She cares too much what others want her to be. She treats us like we're dreams that will fade away. She won't make us real."

Damn them! And damn this whole game! I refuse to argue with myself! This really is insane. I want to run, but I can't make myself move. I'm tired and frustrated – again! I'm sick of it all – again! But it doesn't matter. I'm trapped in my own hamster wheel.

My frustration churns, but who can I be frustrated with? Them? That's laughable. It's been ridiculous since the first day in July when "Lynn" showed up. They taunt me. I hate my lack of control. They bring memories. I want to be left alone. They are more colorful and interesting and rich than I am. They are me. They are not me. Fuck this...!

A gentle hand waves the torment away. My mind calms and my thoughts don't matter anymore. I'm okay now. I'm all right. Things are not as bad as they seem. It's Ruby Red. She is the scent of rose in the warm sun; a child's laughter over still water. She brings a blessing of understanding and peace, like chords of perfect music touching my soul. There is something magnificent about Ruby Red.

"I can explain," she whispers. "It would be better if she weren't so tired, but she needs to know everything. She won't learn how to laugh, play and truly love if we don't help her. Now she uses us as an excuse. She says we are not her – that we are in control, but we all must work together. We want all that she wanted when she was little. We'll give her all the love she's been looking for on the outside. We are her treasures that talk. We are gifts that give back to her."

My mind still doubts. My thoughts still try to justify. But my feelings, my feelings believe in them. There is a powerful force inside me. I am afraid of it, and the changes it could bring if I just let go and give in. I have to leave my friends and go home now. I can't even discuss this with them.

I'm glad it's Sunday. Ruby Red's soothing energy has lasted into this morning, and I'm grateful. I wanted to implode last night and be done with it, but today the game goes on and I try to keep the girls from getting sucked into it. The constant pressure of the guides and all the others keeps us continually with Sean and Molly, and we're with them again this evening. The girls behave more like three sisters now, more than just friends.

As soon as the girls get bored with Sunday night television and head for the basement, I feel a spacey sensation that feels familiar. The room gets bigger and bigger as I sit in the corner of the couch and turn into someone else. Here we go again.

"My name is Montego! Montego is my name!"

Sean and Molly look at each other, preparing for another surprise. This is a new one.

"So, Montego, why have you come to visit?" Molly asks. Tonight she's ready to play with someone new.

"It's my first time!" he blurts. Montego is like Flit. He's very tiny in a very big new world, and he's thrilled to be here.

"It's my first time ever! Peter can't catch us!" he winks. "And I'm not supposed to be here! Peter and Amelia are fun to play with! Did you know we can glow? We make our wings move fast enough to create a light. But Peter and Amelia don't come anymore to our place. We can make lights and color when we flap real fast." I probe to see if I can get some information about why I'm getting this visit and why I think I'm some sort of fairy.

"She should leave me alone!" he complains when he senses my intrusion. "No one tells me what to do! I've waited a long time to come out here! Peter's very big where I live."

I stop probing. Damn it, in spite of myself, this really can be entertaining.

"It's heavy here in your world! We don't see Peter and Amelia anymore. We have to go to a different place to get out. I snuck out!" He looks curiously at Sean and Molly and I have to say that I'm amused at the picture I get from him. They're huge. To Montego they're like chunky circus bears, doing a clumsy dance. He looks down at my arms and legs and tries to flex wings that don't exist. He soon realizes that he is at the mercy of the body he inhabits now.

"We have arms and legs but we also have wings. We wrap them around us to hide and stay dry. We communicate through our wings by moving them up or down and by wrapping them.

Wings are better to communicate with than words are. We use our wings as camouflage. But we get into trouble with each other, because we like to play. We hide and Peter looks for us. Well, he used to when he lived with us." He checks in with me for a second and I get a glimpse of his world. It's much like what I've been shown before: vividly colorful and boundless.

"She is the way in and the way out. The others don't play with us." I know he's talking about the personalities like Liza and Cassie. He is communicating with me somewhat, answering my unspoken questions. I'm curious about his world and hoping to pry some information from him that I can use to give him what he wants and send him back home.

"We can't go see Amelia and Peter," he says with a sad shake of his head. "We can't go there. It's hard to get here, very hard. It's way very far back. Yes, we can see the big white house. We can see it, but no one goes there. It's over the water. But we can see lights around it and glowing out of the windows."

Montego loses his hold and in moments I'm back in my world and everything looks normal. I roll my eyes at Sean and Molly, but I have to smile, too. How can I not be intrigued by some of these little parts? It's interesting to see my internal world come to life, even if it is a world that doesn't really exist.

Cassie visits on and off for the next week, keeping the girls close by and "eating" root beer. Cassie brings my girls back to me. We can share the love and connect with a personality that brings nothing but tenderness and concern for everyone. She's the mother hen who pulls all of us under her wings.

"We're just going to warn her this one time," Cassie clucks. "She is not taking care of herself and it's hard to get through the day. She can't just keep going without concern for us. We won't let her take us down again, to go back to the old way. She relies on old tools. She must not deny us. We come with information. She must get this now. She must admit to who she really is – her flaws and talents.

"She must be true to herself. She always thought she could do it all – but no one can! She can never be good enough by mirroring expectations and having those expectations raised. Then she wonders why she can't win."

Cassie stops for a breath but she isn't done. There is always a message. But Molly and Sean listen closely, because Cassie has always kept their attention. The love that Cassie exudes is compelling and true and her visits are a pleasure. But tonight, with her uncharacteristic passion, they know this is especially important to her.

"The doctor was right when he said her childhood was as stressful as a war zone. We are not criticizing. She did what she had to do to survive and try to be happy. But now there is no one to damage her except herself. Change is in motion. We can't stop it now."

Molly asks Cassie about this big change that's coming.

"We don't know when or how. We don't know if it will affect all or some. Now it's up to her. She doesn't claim us as parts of herself, but we'll break through. She will know us - from the center of herself. But she must take care of herself!"

Finally Cassie is out of energy. She takes one last loving look around and says goodnight to the girls. They give her good, long hugs and send her on her way.

Liza

Your sacred texts and your religions ask you to love. They write the words for you and paint the pictures and preach the meaning. But it is nothing if you do not allow it from within. Love is not in the world unless you place it there. It comes from you, for you. If you do not love, you may see evil in any act. Judgment cannot give love or take it away. The laws of men do not determine destiny. Listen well… love is in all things, all acts, all hearts. If it does not appear to be so, it is your perception that denies it.

Jayd

Each alter was a facet of the ruby, a piece of the puzzle, a step closer to the bridge. Each brought purpose and meaning and always, from the center, love. Rebecca still could not embrace them as parts of herself. Each was an intrusion and foreign. But she learned from them. She felt them. She heard their words and couldn't turn them off. One teaspoon at a time, they fed her love and life and hope. And they would not, could not, give up on the journey. It was all or nothing.

Lynn, Cassie and Liza, the most self-sustained of the personalities, were free from the influence of others. They gave of themselves and let their lights shine. They showed Rebecca how to act instead of react. That it was safe to show love to others without fear of rejection. They loved with abandon and opened her heart to it.

She did not know it yet, but they brought her to the very threshold of the bridge.

The Container

Guides and personalities have analyzed and dissected my thoughts and feelings. They've torn me down, forced me to accept change and are apparently trying to rebuild me. I have changed, but even after the dust settles, how can I not be who I am at the core? I'll still have my memories. I'll still work and clean house and raise my kids. So, why all this effort? I'll be stronger, I suppose. More introspective and insightful, I hope. But why doesn't everyone go through a journey like this? Why am I forced through this rebirth process? So many unanswered questions.

Tonight, in mid-February, I get answers to questions I never thought to ask, and hear how I feel when I never asked to know. My feelings, so obvious to my alters, are a mystery to me until Sean and Molly are available and listening.

"She doesn't want to know who yet remains within her, because she doesn't want them separated, hurt or spoiled. She sacrificed herself long ago to save them. She believes that if she merges with the rest, she will change for the better at the beginning, but eventually she would destroy them. Over time, she will take what they bring and put out their light. She protects them from the world by keeping them safe inside her. She won't let the world do to them what it did to her. She sees them as the only part of herself that is good. But she believes this only at a deeply unconscious level.

"She must understand that the parts are themselves. They can't take over for her. They can't become her. She believes she could harm them and they would be no more. No one there, just emptiness. But they have cleared the way. She knows now that they exist and why they are here. Do you think she can live separately from them and be fulfilled"

The guide leans toward my friends and continues.

"She's afraid she would change them, but also that they would change her. She's afraid of those parts that would do and say things that she wouldn't do or say. That's why she's held herself apart from you. So she can remain emotionally protected and not access the parts she put away. She doesn't want to give up the childhood lessons that she learned so well. If you told her you were tired of her and her problems, she would leave. She doesn't believe she's part of your family. She doesn't believe she belongs anywhere. That is only one of the beliefs that keep her from seeking her treasures."

Is it true that I subconsciously subvert parts of myself and sabotage my healing and my happiness? This is all too hard for me to understand right now. I spend a lot of time confused these days. February has never been an easy month for me. I need sunshine and springtime. February weather here is dark and slushy and cold, and my mind seems to be as frozen right now as the world outside my window.

The End of Rebecca

It's the 21st of February. I've shuffled through the month with little interest in it. Even closing on the new house last week didn't help my mood. And today I feel weak and unsettled. I can't even pinpoint where I feel bad. I just feel bad. This morning it's hard to hold on and stay at work, but I have an appointment with Dr. Allen that I'd rather not miss. I haven't missed one yet. So I plug away at my desk until it's time to leave. Maybe the cold outside will help me snap out of it. Unfortunately, I'm scheduled to come back to work when my appointment is done.

I drop into the doctor's black leather chair as usual, but I really don't feel like talking. Maybe it was a mistake to come here after all. I should have cancelled.

"We have come here today to put Rebecca away," a voice says after a long silence. It sounds like my voice.

"What?" the doctor's brow furrows into a question mark.

"She thought she was the core personality, but she is not. Today we are putting her away." I'm confused, now in the background as usual, but the doctor distracts me when he grabs for his notebook and a pen. He's never done that before. He's never taken notes at all.

"What do you mean? You're 'putting her away'?"

"She thought she was the core personality. She thought all of the alters would merge into her, and she would continue with her life, but this is not to be. She is not the center. She is an alter as well. An alter that was created many years ago to take the pain and become what was expected by her parents and the rest of the world. An alter that deserves respect and honor for what she has accomplished all these years, but an alter nonetheless."

The doctor scribbles, and seems intrigued by this new visitor. I am not so much intrigued as I am terrified. I know they mean what they say, and that I'm not at all in control and haven't been since this all started, but... I'm being put away? Put away where? *What's going on!!*

But I can only think these words. I can't say them. I can't force my way through. I cannot take charge. I can only listen to someone else's words and to the cracking and breaking of the heart that I thought was mine, the pounding of blood through veins that once belonged to me.

"There is no 'I' now. It is done."

We gather loosely together. There is no individual "Rebecca" now and the session is over, with the doctor offering nothing. He has nothing to give us now and we leave his stifling, wooden office and burst into the sunny February chill with our happy secret. Yes, we are free, but we still must live the life, so we drive back to the job. There are obligations and loose ends. We know how to get there. And we know how to do the work. We've all been here every day with her.

When we arrive, there is only an hour left to answer the phone and pretend. Then finally! Out of work and back to Sean and Molly's house.

"Hey, guys! Where are the girls? In Ann's room? Good. Guess what happened today at the doctor's office? You'll never guess! We aren't Rebecca anymore! It's all new now. All the work and all the years and lessons. We made it! We finally made it!!"

They look surprised. They don't get it. Well, they will. They, more than anyone, will understand.

"Rebecca wasn't the truth of us! That was our secret! She was not the heart of us. She was a surrogate, an image, another alter. We're the new way. We are the future and the truth. We want to tell the kids. Where are they? Let's call them in!"

Finally, we're all settled. Everyone is here. God, it's amazing to be doing this. They'll be so excited.

"Guess what? Your mom is dead!"

Damn it, Lynn! What are you doing! Do you always have to be so blunt?!? This is what the girls have been afraid of all along! Will someone else please take charge here?! Now Elizabeth is sobbing and Lee is very angry.

"What do you mean!?" Lee cries. "My Mom is NOT dead!! She is NOT dead! I HATE you!!" Lee leaps up and stalks into the bedroom with Molly behind her.

We shift together inside. We huddle in confusion and guilt. They don't understand that this is good news. It's liberation. But, of course they don't. Lee and Elizabeth haven't done the hard work of the last nine months, the labor of our rebirth. They've met many of us, but in their eyes we did not raise them. *We* did not play with them or stay up all night when they were sick. *We* were not the one always on their side, and by their side. *We* did not wipe their tears or cleanse their scrapes or listen to their secrets. *We* didn't buy their first skates, teach them to ride a bike, or take them to their first school dance.

But we were there, precious ones. Even though you didn't know it. We were always there and we love you, too.

Molly leads Lee back into the living room, but Lee's arms are folded in defiance and tears run down her cheeks. She refuses to sit or to say anything, but her face has crumbled with pain and helplessness. Elizabeth sobs into a pillow as Ann rubs her back and tries to give comfort, but Ann, too, is in tears. Sean sits now, but looks solemn and unsupportive. This is not right. Why isn't it fitting together? How can we explain? What can we do?

Then Cassie surfaces and is stricken with the scorching pain in the room. She doesn't speak, but enters and moves past the rest of us as her perfect love rises to confront the grief. These faces are all dear to her. She doesn't belong to the past. She doesn't carry the pain or the memories. She is here simply to love and be loved. And she does love them. She loves Rebecca's children with a mother's love. And she loves the friends who have given so much and so generously.

So we send through her every expression of love we have ever felt; every sweet sentiment between this mother and her children;

every delicate chord that has ever passed between these friends, and it all pours forth from Cassie in a wrenching, pitiful sob of penitence and distress.

"W-w-w-e di-didn't m-m-mean to hurt anyooonnne!!!"

Cassie's wail carries into the dark night, a desperate plea for forgiveness and understanding. And she has done nothing wrong. No one in this room has done anything wrong, but we have all endured the fire. And Cassie cries for each of us inside this body as well, for our torment and our purpose, but also for our resurrection and our revelations. We are fractured still. We are raw and vulnerable and plead for understanding. We gather together and share the grief, but we possess what her friends and family cannot... the power of experience and the knowledge of this miracle.

We know that creation is painful, and from the ashes of an old identity will come the promise of the future. But how can they know that yet? How can they trust us? Our intent was not to cause more pain, but to correct that which went astray. Huge sacrifice, but many benefits. *Please help us rebuild! Please love us as you loved her...*

Sean wipes his eyes and Molly's cheeks are wet as she hugs Lee. Ann and Elizabeth sob into the big pillows that surround them. Cassie, the sacrifice, sits cross-legged before them and faces the pain squarely while tears drip to her chin, down her neck, and into her collar.

We cannot look at them. Cassie's heart, our heart, breaks with the weight of the pain we have caused this day.

Then, suddenly, the girls are in our arms. Rebecca's daughters, our daughters, who have come to love Cassie, join her now. These young women, who have suffered so much themselves, are willing to give even more. They are part of the bridge, and they are proof that love will always find a way. We hold each other and rock together in mutual support and comfort. Sean and Molly go to Ann as well.

This is the love that can save us. This is the strength that can hold us together while we all heal.

Aftermath

An uncomfortable uneasiness surrounds us today after all of yesterday's emotion. We slept last night, exhausted and with not much resolved. The fallout has begun and our normal routines are shattered. Sean lies unmoving in a sleeping bag near the couch where he spent the night. The girls speak together in muted voices as Molly goes to the kitchen for breakfast. We, the parts, wait. We know how to function. We know how to maneuver through the day. But we are not one yet. We have work to do.

The day passes slowly and no one requires much. No one presses for more. Sean remains in the sleeping bag with his head covered. Molly keeps to herself and finds errands in other parts of the house. The girls recover in Ann's room and only venture out for food. We rest and observe. We wait and do not ask questions.

The next day, Sunday, holds its breath for us. Sean will not speak and his expression warns everyone away. The girls remain in the bedroom. Molly finds a book for escape. But we must communicate today.

Cassie has receded, Lynn does not surface, guides do not explain. But there is still a voice and a beating heart and we must begin anew. We must not continue to mourn that which has been so excruciatingly lost... yet gloriously gained. It *is* a rebirth. It is the truth of us and we must create from it. We've all learned the new lessons. Can we see, eventually, how we've grown? Can we build on what we have learned?

Finally, late in the day, the girls return to the pillows still scattered on the floor. Sean grudgingly surfaces, and Molly is ready to move ahead.

Life goes on, even when everything has changed.

"We have put Rebecca away." We must begin somewhere. "But we honor her journey. She took the pain, did the work, and gave us space to exist. She held a place for us all those years. Her history is ours, and her memories and dreams, and her love for her children. But we must move forward now, filling the whole being as it should have been. We have chosen a new name that includes us all. It is Jayd."

And Jayd had a very slow start. It took weeks, months, for the parts to come together. Three times, in the beginning, Jayd was pulled back into confusion, feeling like tumbled rocks. But we still had the guides to counsel and help us. And we had the continued love of our little family to support us. Molly and Sean still listened. The girls still accepted.

"She's trying to use the old tools," the guides warned. "She cannot create the new path with the old tools."

Our internal processes slowly shifted as Rebecca was gently but firmly integrated with the rest. We fumbled for a while and then moved forward with new ideas and beliefs and choices. There was alternately silliness and melancholy, excitement and trepidation. The honest expression of emotions wasn't easy, but the new path was well monitored by various alters and assorted Others who came and went at will. It took time for Rebecca to understand that she wasn't in control.

As that year went on, I, as Jayd, became increasingly independent with fewer episodes, leaning less on my friends for support and simply enjoying our friendship again. The girls and I nestled into the new house, with the dog and the cat, and opened it up to friends, fun and laughter. We made a happy life for ourselves there as Lee and Elizabeth grew and then moved away to college and their own lives. And, throughout that time, I was able to make good on at least a few of those promises Rebecca had made them.

I have continued through the years to dig deep and to exhume revelations like an archeologist unearths bones. This experience was so rich in treasures that I cannot claim them all. I'm grateful for all I've learned and for who I am because of it. Every day, I use what I was taught.

But I also recognize how my family was victimized by narcissism and narcissistic behavior. I can't minimize the damage that was done and the pain it caused. Growing up with it, and not knowing any other way, made it an insidious burden to bear and very daunting to confront. Seeking deeper meaning within the struggle was the best way for me to make sense of any of it. Asking for peace was the powerful first step. Letting go was the challenge.

When you begin to awaken to your inner voice, however it may express, change will be inevitable. Remember to ask for help - and have faith that it will come. If support is available, make sure you accept it. You don't have to find your bridge alone.

Liza

You do not need to leave this world to find your bridge. You do not need to break into pieces, bringing alters and guides. Just make room for more than your five senses can give you. Let your heart and your intuitive knowing lead you to the deeper meaning of what you see and hear and touch. You are not limited by your earthly vision. You are so much greater.

Jayd

I believe Liza. And I believe *in* her. She isn't locked inside my mind as a memory. She is a part of me, as are multitudes of others, as you have read.

Liza and I don't ask you to believe in our journey. We don't ask you to believe in anything except yourself. And we offer no final explanations. We wouldn't do that to you, because they don't exist, and we don't need or want them anyway. We're too busy enjoying our exploration of life. We want that for you, too, because it's magical and amazing.

You may wonder at this point what is within you. What exists inside that vast soul and vivid imagination with which you were gifted? Where are you, who are you, beneath the layer upon layer of worldly imprinting? And there may be a million more questions beyond these. I hope so. Whatever else you do in your life, keep asking them. But ask them of yourself. Seek your own truth and pay attention to what rises from within. And be willing to sit in the empty bliss of not-knowing.

Find your bridge by letting go. It's the easiest way to get there.

CPSIA information can be obtained
at www.ICGtesting.com
Printed in the USA
FFOW05n1749020615

9 781504 332316